A CUP OF COFFEE WITH

10 OF THE TOP PERSONAL
INJURY ATTORNEYS IN THE UNITED STATES

VALUABLE INSIGHTS YOU
SHOULD KNOW BEFORE
YOU SETTLE YOUR CASE

Randy V. Pelham, Esq.
Randy Van Ittersum

Rutherford Publishing House
PO Box 969
Ramseur, NC 27316
www.RutherfordPublishingHouse.com

Cover photo: Mi.Ti./Bigstock.com
Cover photo: -Markus-/Bigstock.com

ISBN-10: 0692437304
ISBN-13: 978-0692437308

TABLE OF CONTENTS

ACKNOWLEDGEMENTS

We all want to thank our husbands and wives, fathers and mothers, and everybody who has played a role in shaping our lives and our attitudes.

To all the clients we've had the honor of working with, who shaped our understanding of the difficulty of this time for you and your families. It has been our privilege to serve each and every one of you.

INTRODUCTION

Contributing Author:

Randy Van Ittersum

Host & Founder – Business Leader Spotlight Show

A s the host for the Business Leader Spotlight Show, I had the pleasure to interview over two hundred and fifty personal injury attorneys to bring our listeners valuable insights that they should know about before they settle their claim. The personal injury attorneys that were interviewed are considered the leading personal injury attorneys in the country, and the information they shared about personal injury claims was eye opening.

When I decided to write and publish this book, I wanted to bring to my readers the insights from the best personal injury attorneys that I interviewed on the show. I am pleased to bring you the thoughts of the 10 best personal injury attorneys out of the top 250 attorneys interviewed. These ten personal injury attorneys come from different areas of the country, where the laws pertaining to personal injury cases might vary slightly, but each co-author discusses valuable opinions about the challenges that you may face with your claim if you have been seriously injured.

Introduction

Personal injury attorneys play a critical role in making our lives safer. By holding companies and individuals accountable for defective products or negligent conduct, they make businesses and people think about their actions. Without accountability, a higher number of people would be injured or die, leaving their loved ones devastated by the actions of another person.

No-one ever asks to be injured, but when they are involved in a serious accident, caused by another party's negligent conduct, a personal injury attorney is there to help them repair their life. A serious accident will cause you to lose time at work thereby affecting your ability to meet your financial obligations. The injuries that you incur will certainly affect the quality of your life, for at least a short period of time, while you recover, and may affect the quality of your life until the day you die. Although a personal injury attorney can't cure you physically, they can help to repair your life financially, and get you the recompense required to compensate you for your lost wages, pain, and suffering.

If you have been involved in an accident and are injured by another party, you will be dealing with one or more insurance companies. It could be the insurance company covering the party that caused the injury, or it might be your own insurance company. When I was interviewing personal injury attorneys on the Business Leader Spotlight Show, one thing stood out above everything else: If insurance companies treated you fairly, when it comes to settling your claim, personal injury attorneys would be out of business.

Unfortunately, as was the opinion of every personal injury attorney I interviewed, insurance companies are focused on their profits; therefore, their motivation is to settle a claim for as little an amount as possible. As a result, if you are in a serious accident, you will need an advocate who will fight for your rights to ensure you get you the compensation you deserve.

When I interviewed these professionals, they repeatedly told me that most people that come to them say that they never expected they would ever have to hire a lawyer. They shared that most people are embarrassed when they come into their office, because it's just not in their nature to sue anybody. But they had to see someone because they needed help. They discovered and felt that the insurance company just wasn't dealing fairly with them.

I equate it to a David and Goliath situation. On one side you have an insurance company who has vast resources, an army of attorneys, and highly trained insurance adjusters who are trying to settle the claim for as little as possible. And there is nothing wrong with that because they usually represent the party that caused the accident. On the other side you have the injured party, who is hurting both physically and financially, and most likely has never been in a serious accident before and had to deal with an insurance company. The personal injury attorney is your David who has the knowledge and resources to stand up to your Goliath, the insurance company. Your personal injury attorney is your advocate and is there to protect you.

Another thing I discovered when interviewing these attorneys was the sooner a client contacts an attorney, the better it will be for their case. One reason for this is that, often, it is important they get an investigator to the scene of the accident to preserve evidence that might be critical to their case. Another reason is so they can protect the client from being contacted and interviewed by the insurance adjuster from the opposing insurance company.

Every personal injury attorney I interviewed shared the fact that insurance adjusters are highly trained and want to get a recorded statement from you. And although they may appear to be befriending you, the only thing they want is to get you to say something that can damage your case and help them settle your claim for the least amount possible. Once you hire an attorney, they can't contact you without first going through your attorney. The fact is, most injured parties want to be cooperative and tell their side of the story hoping that it will help them settle their case quickly. Unfortunately, they often say, innocently, something that will be used against them to minimize their settlement.

It became crystal clear to me that if you are ever in a serious accident, you need to contact a personal injury attorney as quickly as possible. One attorney I interviewed had been a claim adjuster for thirty years before he passed the bar and became a personal injury attorney. There were two important facts that he shared. One was that the insurance company he represented set aside higher reserves whenever a personal injury attorney was hired by the injured party. The second was that the insurance companies track and rate the personal injury attorneys across the country. They know who settles quickly and who is willing to go to trial, if necessary, to get a fair settlement. The bottom line is that when you hire a personal injury attorney who is willing to take your case to trial, 90% of the time you will be offered a settlement, but for a much larger sum than an attorney that isn't willing to go to trial.

The fact is this; if you are injured in an accident you should hire the best personal injury attorney that you can find. The legal profession has actually created a system that makes the courts accessible to everyone, regardless of whether they are rich or poor. Almost all personal injury attorneys are paid with what is known as a contingency fee. This means that they do not get paid unless they settle your case, or win a judgment, if you go to trial. They in effect have skin in the game, and put their time and money at risk to secure the best possible outcome for you. If they don't settle your case or lose at trial, they get nothing.

Furthermore, almost all personal injury attorneys will meet with you for free. This means that you can sit down and talk to an attorney about your case and it doesn't cost you anything. Because almost all personal injury attorneys charge the same percentage under the contingency fee agreement, there is absolutely no reason that you shouldn't hire the best personal injury attorney you can find.

As I pointed out in the beginning, I have interviewed over two hundred and fifty of the top personal injury attorneys in the country. The ten attorneys I asked to co-author this book, are the best of the best. In fact, if I lived near any one of these attorneys and was seriously injured in an accident, I would hire them in a heartbeat.

When you hire a personal injury attorney, you are likely to build a lifelong personal relationship with that person. They are your lifeline to help you repair your life. You will have friends and family that will do all they can to help you through this difficult period of your life, but it will be your attorney that will help you be compensated for the quality of life that you have lost due to the negligent conduct of another.

It doesn't matter how you got this book, whether you purchased it or it was given to you, it is filled with golden nuggets of information that you need to know if you or a family member have been injured in a serious accident. The information contained within this book can be critical to finding and identifying the best attorney to help you get the settlement you deserve. In fact I would go so far as to say that no insurance company wants you to read this book.

Randy Van Ittersum
Host & Founder – Business Leader Spotlight Show

1

DON'T BELIEVE INSURANCE TELEVISION COMMERCIALS

by Randy V. Pelham, Esq.

Randy V. Pelham, Esq.
The Pelham Law Firm
Tallahassee, Florida

Randy understands first-hand what an accident victim goes through. Prior to becoming a personal injury attorney he was a police officer in Miami, and was injured in the line of duty due to the negligence of another driver. His personal experience has piloted him to have an uncommon concern for people who have been injured by the negligence, carelessness, and recklessness of others. His care and compassion when working with people who have been injured in an accident, is one of the reasons why he has so many satisfied and loyal clients. He seeks justice and a fair settlement for each victim and understands the importance of staying in touch with his clients and communicating the progress of one's case as it goes through the claims and legal process.

DON'T BELIEVE INSURANCE TELEVISION COMMERCIALS

This is the first thing that comes to mind when someone asks me why it would be necessary to hire a personal injury attorney: insurance television commercials. Commercials by the "Good Hands People" or the ones featuring a happy, talking lizard are designed to make individuals think that insurance companies are good and they will take care of injured victims. However, the fact is that an insurance company is there to take care of those who are their insured. In my experience, insurance companies are not looking out for the best interests of the injured person, whether that person is their own insured customer or the opposing party. Even when the injured party is the customer who has been involved in an accident with an uninsured driver, or a driver without adequate insurance coverage, insurance companies are protecting themselves—whether or not the customer has underinsured or uninsured coverage included in the policy. In that example, the injured person may be placed in an adversarial position even though it is his own insurance company that should be taking care of him, and might need a personal injury attorney to protect his rights.

Some insurance adjusters aggressively contact the injured party after a vehicle accident, sometimes in the immediate aftermath of the incident, hoping to obtain a settlement before the person can seek the counsel of a personal injury attorney. The insurance adjuster will try to convince the injured person that his claim is worth "X" amount of dollars and that the adjuster can pay him immediately if he is willing to settle. Some even use phrases such as, "An attorney will take one-third of your money." Substantial training from the insurance company gives the insurance adjuster a superior position of knowledge about the claim's worth, versus the average person who does not work in the industry and has not dealt with personal injury claims. In order to even out the playing field, an injured person needs a personal injury attorney who will protect his rights and ensure a fair settlement.

As I have evaluated personal injury cases during my years of practice, one thing stands out: no two cases are alike. Cases vary as much as people do, and there is no secret formula one can use to determine if a neck injury is worth "X" amount of money or a knee injury is worth "X" amount of money. Each case is unique to that particular person in that particular accident. This is why I highly recommend at least one meeting with a personal injury attorney to anyone who suffers an injury, so that he or she is on the same footing as the insurance company.

A few years ago I was fortunate to discover part of an Allstate training manual with information from a 1995 study, revealing that people who were represented by a personal injury attorney typically received three times the settlement amount than a person who settled without an attorney. Even before I happened upon that study, I knew it was true, from my meetings with people who disclosed to me the difference between what the insurance company had offered them and what I had helped them to receive when the case was tried or settled. Sometimes, people contact me after it's too late for me to help them. One woman contacted me several years ago after she was told by an insurance adjuster that her case was worth $5,000 and "why share any of that with an attorney, because that is all your case is worth." She accepted the settlement and then needed surgery. Her case was actually worth well into six figures, but there was nothing I could do at that point, since she had settled the claim in full for $5,000.

For all of these reasons, an injured party should at least try to get a legal opinion before considering a case settlement with an insurance company. In my experience, most personal injury attorneys work on a contingency basis, which means they don't get paid until and unless they negotiate or win a settlement for the client. Therefore, there is no risk for the individual to hire an attorney. If the lawyer does not get a settlement then no payment is required. In these cases, the injured party receives the benefit of an experienced personal injury attorney working to protect their rights, and the injured party assumes no risk for paying the attorney unless money is received from the insurance company.

I'VE BEEN WHERE YOU ARE

I not only practice personal injury law, I have been on the other side of the table when I was injured at work. Before I went to law school, I worked for the City of Miami Police Department. I entered the Academy in 1982 and then went to work for the city. In 1989, I made the decision to enter law school, so I worked during the day and attended law school in the evenings. In 1991, another driver ran a stop sign and hit the side of my police car. Even though I had injured my back, I had just begun my last year of law school and didn't want to pursue a claim that might interfere with my legal studies. To complicate matters further, I was paying my way through law school by working for the City during the day and taking off-duty police jobs for private employers, such as supermarkets and nightclubs. Miami's policy states that if you are injured, you cannot take any side jobs. That income was vital for my ability to put food on my table, pay for law school, and take care of my family.

I tried to ignore the injury and did not immediately contact an attorney about the accident. In my case, the insurance companies ignored me rather than aggressively pursuing me for a quick settlement. I believe they tried to pretend I did not exist. After several weeks, I realized that the pain was not going away, and I needed a doctor because I had been injured on the job. I began the worker's compensation process and the City sent me to their doctors. At the time, I had no idea that one doctor might favor an insurance company or an employer while another doctor would act in the best interests of his patient, no matter what situation brought that patient into his office. Now that I practice personal injury law, I designate doctors as patient-oriented or insurance-oriented, and have an idea as to which party will be favored by the doctor in a personal injury case. A third set of doctors are basically "hired guns" because whichever party sees them first is the one they will try to help out during the case.

Unfortunately, when I was injured, I didn't understand any of these concepts. Of course, the City sent me to 'insurance doctors' to examine me. At the time, I was muscular and in pretty good physical shape from weight-lifting. Those doctors took one look at me and thought, "You do not appear to be injured, and you went back to work as a cop – everything must be okay," so they dismissed me. I saw more doctors, but none would listen to me when I explained that I was in pain. I complained to the person handling my worker's compensation claim that the doctors weren't listening to me, but nothing came from those complaints.

After six months, someone suggested that I hire an attorney. The first attorney I met with explained to me that these doctors were 'insurance doctors' or 'employer doctors', who would say whatever would help the insurance company or the employer regardless of my physical health. These doctors failed to perform diagnostic tests that would have revealed my injury. With the help of my attorney, constant complaints, and after finally filing legal documents, at last the worker's compensation company sent me to a competent surgeon. During my first appointment with the surgeon, he ordered diagnostic tests that revealed my need for back surgery. I suffered through much unnecessary pain, frustration, and wasted time before I was finally seen by a competent doctor that was more worried about me than about who was padding his wallet.

That entire journey required four different attorneys before everything was settled. I would also like to add that there are many doctors who are dedicated, experienced physicians that know what they are doing. In a non-legal setting, they will probably do a very good job for you. It is just unfortunate that some doctors make a lot of money by receiving referrals from insurance companies, which might encourage them to neglect to invest in proper testing or treatment for their patients.

I TREAT YOU THE WAY I WOULD WANT TO BE TREATED

Going back to the different ways lawyers handle cases, I can only speak from my experience with lawyers in Florida, Georgia, and Alabama. Most of these attorneys work on a contingency basis, so they are only paid if they negotiate or win a settlement for their client. They will receive a percentage of that settlement as compensation for their services. There is a lot of variance in how an attorney can handle a case within the parameters of state law. The way I handle a case may not be the same way another attorney handles a case. I am not saying that the other attorney is wrong and that I am correct, it's just the way that I prefer to handle my cases. I treat my clients the way I wanted to be treated as a client. I am not perfect, and I would be lying if I said 100% of my clients were completely satisfied and liked me by the end of a case. However, I am fortunate to have a high percentage of clients that are very happy with how I have handled their cases.

In order to give you an idea of how a personal injury case is handled, I will illustrate the way I handle a case under Florida law. In Florida, as in many other states, a personal injury attorney receives a percentage of the settlement if he settles the case prior to a lawsuit being filed. If a lawsuit is filed, then the attorney receives an increased percentage. In Florida, it is generally 33.3% pre-suit and 40% if a lawsuit is filed. In my practice, and from what I have read about Florida statistics in general, between 90% and 95% of personal injury cases settle pre-suit. Therefore, in my office, a lawsuit is only filed in less than 10% of my personal injury cases.

My general rule is to file a lawsuit as a last resort. There are exceptions to that rule, such as preservation of evidentiary matters or when a statute of limitations is about to expire. I find that pre-suit cases settle more quickly than those for which you are required to file a lawsuit. Unfortunately, some attorneys will file a lawsuit as soon as the client hires them. In the absence of a valid reason to do so, the attorney is actually giving himself a "pay raise" by filing the lawsuit without trying to first settle the claim. The clients are simply relying on their attorney's advice when told that they must file suit right away, and never question why this must be done.

Although personal injury attorneys may all handle cases a little differently, they should all be there to protect their client's interests. In my case, I had to hire and fire three attorneys before I found one that I liked, because they would not tell me what was going on with my case, and I wanted to know what my attorney was doing for me. The previous attorneys seemed to act as if my file was "top secret" and therefore could not share it with me. Similar to doctors who keep you from thumbing through your medical file, the attorneys did not want to show me what they were doing to protect my interests and settle my case. It is my belief that a client and a patient have the right to look through their own records.

Since I feel this way, I send my clients a copy of everything pertaining to their case, so that they know exactly what I am doing on their behalf. I also make it a point to schedule a conference with my clients so that we can sit down, go through their file and discuss their case—we work as a team to achieve a successful outcome. While some clients want to be even more involved in their case, which is fine, some clients do not need or want me to do this with them. Furthermore, I believe that clients should have some say or the final say in whether or not a lawsuit is filed, especially if the client must pay the opposing counsel's attorney's fees and costs on a lost trial (as is the rule in Florida). In several cases, I thought we had a better than average chance of winning and wanted to take the case to trial, but the client did not wish to assume the risk and thus, accepted a lower settlement. This was the client's choice and his right, as he was the injured party assuming the risk of going to trial.

In my opinion, a personal injury attorney should do the following things for his clients: handle the case in his client's best interest, give his client all of the options with pros and cons, and provide sound legal advice so that the client can make an informed decision within their comfort zone. The process should be similar to working with a financial planner. You do not want to work with a financial planner who acts like a dictator by taking all of your money, making investments, and failing to explain to you the risks involved with those investments.

THE INSURANCE COMPANY IS YOUR ADVERSARY

Going back to how an injured person is placed in an adversarial position with the insurance company, it is because insurance companies are looking out for their corporation's bottom line of profit. Regardless of how nice an insurance adjuster may seem with the confidence-building "friendly tactic," it is his job to resolve the claim for as little money as possible. One insurance company in particular is currently trying to "starve out" the plaintiff's attorneys by arguing every fact and fighting every claim so that it becomes too expensive for these attorneys to take claims associated with that company. The insurance company believes that the plaintiff's attorneys will then automatically settle or turn down cases with which the company is affiliated, because it is too expensive to fight the case in court. This company is treating all cases in this manner whether the injured party is a customer or not.

It is important for people to understand that a "we're on the same team" type of relationship doesn't exist with an insurance company, because its goal is to settle the claim for as little as possible and save as much money as possible in the process. I do wish to emphasize that even though it is an adversarial position, attorneys are generally polite and friendly when they deal with other parties in the case. Clients have come to me after meeting with another attorney and said they suspected that the insurance company was paying him because he was so friendly with the adjuster. I have never heard even a rumor that an attorney was being paid by an insurance company to cheat his client. Nevertheless, clients believe what they see on television and in movies, and expect to see attorneys screaming, shouting, and throwing things at the opposing side. For the most part, we are cordial and friendly; however, personal injury attorneys are bulldogs when it's necessary to protect their clients. The ultimate goal in a personal injury case is to get just and fair compensation for the client, but it must still be accomplished within the framework of a risk-involved situation. An old saying about personal injury cases goes something like this: "A good settlement is one where both parties are unhappy. The plaintiff is unhappy because he thinks he should have gotten more money, and the insurance company is unhappy because they paid more than they wanted to pay." Basically, a good settlement is one in which both parties compromise to reach a fair and just settlement figure.

In my time as an officer for the City of Miami, I was in four different riots during the '80s, and I saw my share of chaos and crime in the midst of those riots. There were moments on the streets of Miami when I needed to be friendly and laugh with the bad guy so that I could arrest him without further harm to him, other citizens, or myself. Then there were times when I had to be the bad guy just like him so that I was on his level and could intimidate him into doing what I wanted him to do.

I think the same holds true when in an adversarial position with an insurance company. There is a time for me to be nice, during the pre-suit, when honey attracts more flies than vinegar. Therefore, I will joke with certain adjusters that I have worked with on a consistent basis over the years. We are friendly even though we both understand that we are on opposing sides. I keep everything very cordial, which usually helps me to negotiate better settlements for my clients. An insurance attorney once told me that the adjuster was willing to settle at a higher rate because he appreciated dealing with me, as I was not antagonistic, condescending, or angry with him. Sometimes this tactic is beneficial and others times it is not; some adjusters will not change their position no matter how nice you are. Once I file a lawsuit, the time for being nice is generally over. It reminds me of Patrick Swayze's instructions as head bouncer in Road House: "You will be nice until I decide it's time not to be nice." While there is always an adversarial relationship with the insurance company, it is handled differently at different moments in the process.

WHAT IS YOUR CASE WORTH?

Deciding the worth of a case is a complex issue associated with personal injury cases. Some attorneys will tell clients that their case is worth hundreds of thousands of dollars, or that it is the best personal injury case they have ever seen, in order to entice clients to hire them as their attorney. I tell people during the first meeting that I have no idea how much their case is worth today because I have settled cases involving a herniated disc in the neck—a pretty serious injury—for as low at $10,000 to as high as $500,000, and everywhere in between. An attorney must take many factors into account: the client's age and health prior to the accident, the mechanics of the accident, the type of accident, and other forces causing the injury. It is almost impossible to tell a client in the very first visit how much his case is worth.

Additional elements surrounding the client's life can affect the worth of a claim: the client's educational background and expertise level, whether or not the client was working when the accident occurred, or the client's plans for the future. For example, I have a new client who injured her pinkie so seriously that she cannot bend it. It is crooked and stuck in one position. For most people, that may not be a debilitating injury, but because my client is a pianist, this injury is very significant and traumatic. I must consider her age to determine how many more years she would have been working had this injury not occurred. For others, the assessment may include how the injury affects their current job, their ability to get future raises and promotions, or the ability to move to a different industry where their background and education would be valuable in terms of salary and benefits. Questions abound. Will this person need to be retrained? How will the injury impact his personal life? Will he become totally disabled due to the injury? A personal injury attorney must examine each of these factors and others before determining the worth of any particular personal injury claim.

Location is another factor that determines case value. It matters where the injury occurred and in what locale the case will be tried, because political beliefs can play a significant role in how a case is decided. For instance, while Leon County in Tallahassee is primarily a Democratic voting district, the county is considered very conservative when it comes to lawsuits. Therefore, a jury in Leon County will award a lower amount for a particular injury than a jury would in the next northern county (Gadsden), which is very liberal. This plays a large role in our negotiations with insurance companies, who have already charted out the various counties and know which ones award higher and lower amounts to claimants. In a rural setting, someone with a traumatic injury might only receive between $50,000 and $100,000 because the jury considers that to be a huge amount of money. However, in another jurisdiction, the jury may realize that the injury is worth much more and award $500,000.

A personal injury attorney must know and manage many case details: the politics of the county in which the case will be tried, the effect of the psychology of the jury on the verdict amount, the client's medical care, etc. The attorney must stay on top of the doctors' reports, know which diagnostic tests are being done, and review those results. If certain diagnostic tests are not performed to reveal all of the injuries, cases may settle before the client discovers that he has a more serious injury than he assumed. It's risky to settle too quickly without all of the information. Before settling any case, I must look over the medical records, ensure that all medical tests were completed, review those results, and follow up with specialists if necessary because future medical treatment plays a big role in determining the value of a claim. Determining the value of a claim is thus much more complex than simply stating, "You have a neck injury that is worth $5,000."

BEWARE OF THESE LANDMINES

Landmines occasionally blow up in a personal injury case, due to lack of photos, witnesses, physical evidence, or recorded statements. For example, any time someone is injured, you need to preserve as much evidence as possible before the evidence is moved. In an automobile accident, this means taking pictures of the cars with your phone or someone else's phone, getting witness information, and so forth. For many people, taking pictures is the last thing on their mind after an auto accident. Things and memories have a tendency to change, so having this evidence is important if the case goes to trial. In Florida, an officer can testify as to what he saw at the accident, but his report cannot be entered into evidence. So, it is important for clients to try to preserve the scene, if possible.

Another example worth considering is a slip-and-fall case at a store. There are many things that I will need to know in order to pursue a claim: what you slipped on, whether it was liquid, whether there was dirt in the liquid indicating that it had been there for a while, whether the store's warning signs were clearly visible, etc. Since the store will clean the scene, it is important to document as much evidence and information as possible when the incident occurs.

Unfortunately, when a client comes to me several weeks or even months after an accident has occurred, it is too late to go back to preserve the evidence. Cars may have been repaired and accident scenes have been cleaned. In auto accidents, I must then request pictures from the insurance company, which are not always easy to get pre-suit. In slip-and-fall cases, I am rarely able to get anything from the store's surveillance system, as it was either not on or the tape has already been reused. The few times I have seen a store's security tape, it has usually helped the store more than my client. The more a client can do to preserve the scene of their accident, no matter what kind it is, the more it will help the case. Take pictures of any visible marks, such as bruising, blisters, or cuts, before they are treated and have time to heal. Lack of preserved evidence is a landmine routinely discovered by attorneys.

A recorded statement can also be a big landmine, especially if it has been given to an insurance company for later use against the client. For example, if your testimony changes even slightly, the attorney for the insurance company is going to spin that to make it sound as if you are lying or at least not being completely honest and forthright. This is why it is so important for people to discuss their rights with an attorney immediately following an accident. I have allowed my clients to give non-recorded statements to an insurance adjuster while I was present in the room to object to any inappropriate questions. The interviews are not recorded, so it is much more difficult to twist what is said. By the time most clients contact me, they have already given a recorded statement. When I remind them of what they said I hear, "I did not mean it that way!" Unfortunately, we are now stuck with this landmine that might explode at any moment. It is very difficult to change one's statement and yet remain credible with a jury.

Social media is a cheap, easy surveillance tool for insurance companies that has recently become a potential landmine for personal injury cases. Insurance attorneys know that Facebook, Twitter, and an array of other sites allow people to plaster pictures and videos across the Internet without thinking. Even things that are meant to be private have a way of ending up on a public profile page. People want to look nice in pictures, so they smile, even when they are in serious pain. Maybe they already had a vacation scheduled and they simply want to go, relax, and heal, but someone inadvertently posts a picture of them lying on a beach chair, sunning themselves by the ocean. Now, what is the attorney for the insurance company going to do with those videos and photos? He will download them, show them to the jury, and say, "Look, he is not in any pain. Don't you wish you could go on vacation after a serious accident? Here is another picture six months after the accident. He does not appear to be in pain, does he?" What the jury is thinking at this point may not be very good for the case. This is why I inform clients, in bold ink, to get rid of Facebook and all social media when they hire me. I inform them that they must not post any pictures from that point forward, because it will be taken out of context.

Here is another perfect example of the social media landmine. I had a client, a very attractive young lady, who was attending Florida State University when she suffered a pretty severe back injury. She loved to go out dancing with her friends, and felt very depressed that she could not do so because of her injury. One evening, she went out with her friends, had a few drinks, and posted about 30 pictures of her, dancing and jumping around. Of course, the alcohol probably lessened the pain; nevertheless, she was dancing, laughing, and smiling in all of the pictures. At the beginning of each case, I file a Request for Production of Documents that asks, in part, if the other party has any pictures involving the incident. The opposing counsel responded that they did not have any pictures, and at the time, my client had not yet posted them. However, prior to the trial, the opposing counsel found my client's Facebook page with all of her pictures posted for everyone to see. Four weeks before the trial, I received a pre-trial form showing all of these pictures that would now be used as evidence against my client. At that point, it was too late for me to do anything. In this case, as in others, there is usually a way for the opposing side to find damaging information. So, in those cases, I may choose to show this information to the jury myself in an attempt to mitigate the damages. Whether it is a previous arrest record or a group of photos, I present it to the jury before the other side has a chance to do so. This way, I can explain the context before the opposing counsel tries to impeach my client's credibility.

YOUR INITIAL CONSULTATION – DO YOU HAVE A CASE?

A personal injury case begins with an initial consultation, so that I can get a general idea of the basics of the case. Some attorneys are what I call "super exhaustive" in their initial consultation. They may keep the clients there for two or more hours to get each and every detail, down to the smallest, so that they can make a decision right away as to whether or not they will take the case. I handle my consultations a bit differently. I do not look at the monetary value of the case as some attorneys do, who just want the big-dollar cases. Rather, I look at the "meat" of why this client has come to see me. I believe we are here to help people, so I look at two things during the consultation: negligence and injury. If the client caused his own injury, I cannot help him, but if the negligence of someone else is to blame for my client's injury, I can.

It's also important to ask if the client was actually injured. A man came to meet with me several years ago, and upon asking him whether he was injured, he informed me that he was not. I then asked why he was there to see me. The man stated that someone had told him that if he came to see me, I would send him to a doctor who would say he was injured and then we could both get some money. I explained that what he was suggesting was not just criminal fraud, it was also immoral in my opinion. These are the types of individuals who cause news programs to air segments that sensationalize fraud in the personal injury area. I told him to leave my office immediately.

In my practice, if a person is injured, even it is a minor injury, I am willing to help. During the initial consultation, we vet the simple facts of the case, such as the date of the accident and the other details. The date is important to protect the time period from running out under the statute of limitations, which varies from state to state. I think Tennessee's is one of the shortest, allowing maybe one year from the date of the accident to settle or file a lawsuit. Florida's statute of limitations allows four years for most personal injury actions, and Georgia's allows two years.

Attorneys also look at the other party involved in the case to determine if there is a conflict of interest in taking the case (i.e. I know the other party, I represented the other party in another case, I know the owner of the company, etc.). I will also find out if there are any pictures of, or witnesses to, the accident. This information is the "meat" that will allow us to begin working on the case. I do not need to see every medical report or read every insurance letter before making a decision to take it on. After I have taken it, I give notice of my representation to the other parties and notify the insurance company that the injured party is represented by counsel. I am looking for the pertinent facts that tell me right off the bat whether I have a case, who the opposition is, and how much time is left for negotiations before a lawsuit must be filed.

PURCHASE ADEQUATE INSURANCE FOR YOURSELF

I would like to talk about insurance in general. In Florida, many people do not carry what is called uninsured or underinsured motorist coverage because it's not the state's mandatory requirement. Many people may assume that they have this type of motorist coverage because they have full coverage when in reality they do not, because it is considered to be voluntary extra coverage. The purpose of uninsured and underinsured motorist coverage is to cover the gaps of an at-fault driver's insurance. For example, if you are involved in an automobile accident with a person who has minimum coverage, but your injuries and the damage to your car far exceed minimum coverage, you are left with substantial bills. However, if you carry under-insured coverage, your own insurance company "stands in" and compensates you for your damages and injuries. If the driver had no insurance and you have uninsured coverage, the same would be true—your insurance company would pay for your damages and injuries.

I had a young girl as a client once whose hip had been broken, and required surgery to insert an artificial hip. The at-fault driver was insured for $10,000. Unfortunately, my client did not have underinsured coverage so we could only collect $10,000, far below the amount that should have been paid for this type of injury. Therefore, I tell all of my clients to carry the highest level of insurance protection that they can afford on their liability policy as well as an additional uninsured and underinsured policy. Since people are trying to save money, they reduce their liability insurance to the state's minimum coverage. Underinsured motor coverage thus becomes very important if you are in an accident with someone who only has the state's minimum coverage. I strongly recommend purchasing under-insured and uninsured motorist coverage.

There is a safety issue I would also like to discuss that deals with children as passengers in the front seat. Parents, including some of my own friends, often put their seven- to ten-year-old children in the front passenger seat without a booster seat or car seat, never considering that side passenger airbags might cause them to be severely injured. In an accident, these airbags are deployed at 200 miles an hour toward your child. Many years ago, a woman was taking her eight-year-old daughter to school. A 15-year old non-licensed driver who was taking his sibling to school at his parents' request had a minor collision with my client. It put a very small dent in the bumper of my client's car (less than $200 in damage), but it was enough to cause the airbag to deploy. My client's daughter, who had been seated in the front passenger seat, broke her neck and was paralyzed from the neck down because of the airbag. Too many people ignore warnings about the dangers that airbags pose to smaller children, so I urge my clients and anyone who will listen to keep anyone under the age of 13 in the back seat for their own safety. A child will be much safer in the back seat of a vehicle than in the front seat.

In summary, I would advise everyone to consult with a personal injury attorney in the event that they are involved in an accident or are injured in some way. The most important factor in a personal injury case is that you have confidence in your attorney, and are comfortable with the way they'll handle your case. Some people are intimidated by attorneys or believe that they must do whatever an attorney advises them to do, but I am here to tell you that this is not true. The attorney is working for you, and you should have some input as to how your case is handled. I may not allow clients to tell me how to handle their case, but I also do not force them into taking any action that makes them uncomfortable. I tell each of my clients, "I don't like losing clients, and it hurts my feelings when I do, but if you're not happy with me, find a lawyer that you're confident in and comfortable with because this is your only case." An attorney has hundreds of cases, but that is the client's only case. The client really needs to ensure that they will be represented by someone whom they trust to work in their best interests.

(This content should be used for informational purposes only. It does not create an attorney-client relationship with any reader and should not be construed as legal advice. If you need legal

advice, please contact an attorney in your community who can assess the specifics of your situation.)

2

DON'T HIRE A BASKETBALL COACH TO LEAD A FOOTBALL TEAM

by Sam Aguiar, Esq.

Sam Aguiar, Esq.
Aguiar Injury Lawyers, PLLC
Louisville, Kentucky

Sam is the CEO of Aguiar Injury Lawyers. At 28 years old, Sam was designated in the Kentucky Trial Court Review as the second most prolific trial attorney in Kentucky for that year. Sam's experience and belief in "world class customer service" has allowed him to grow Aguiar Injury Lawyers into comprehensive teams that have all learned his methods and approaches to handling all personal injury cases with speed, aggressiveness, and responsiveness. In turn, Aguiar Injury Lawyers has developed a uniquely effective process that creates a sense of unity between the firm and its client base that allows them to unite and take on the insurance companies together. Sam Aguiar is a member of the Louisville Bar Association, Kentucky Bar Association and the American Association for Justice. In 2013 Sam was named to the National Trial Lawyers: Top 100 Trial Lawyers as well as their Top 40 Under 40.

DON'T HIRE A BASKETBALL COACH TO LEAD A FOOTBALL TEAM

I am a huge sports fan, and many of the analogies I make are related to sports. One analogy that I often use with friends and family is that of a basketball coach who has taken his team to the Sweet Sixteen, Elite Eight, Final Four, or even to the National Championship several times. Locally, Rick Pitino comes to mind. He certainly has a gift for coaching players: helping them to master their talents and excel in their sport. However, you cannot take this wonderful basketball coach, put him in front of the school's football team, and tell him, "Okay, you did a great job coaching our basketball team, so now is your chance to really shine and take our football program to the next level. Go win the BCS title." The basketball coach is going to look at you as if you are crazy. He knows that if he accepts the job, he will inevitably fail, and on the field, the team will look similar to Scott Bakula and Kathy Ireland's team of Texas State in the 1991 movie, *Necessary Roughness.*

This analogy applies to the position of personal injury attorneys. We work in a very dedicated, specialized, and specific field of law. I often tell my friends, "If you receive a citation for a DUI at three o'clock in the morning, you can certainly give me a call, but it would probably be the worst legal decision you have ever made." As a personal injury attorney, I have no experience in handling DUI cases. Similarly, if a man or woman who receives traumatic brain and spinal injuries in an accident decides to hire a famous criminal attorney, a divorce attorney, or even an attorney who drafts the best contracts in the state, no one can deny that he has certainly hired a great attorney, but he has also hired one who likely lacks the requisite knowledge and skill set to handle this type of case.

INSURANCE ADVERTISING IS NOTHING LIKE THE REAL WORLD OF INSURANCE CLAIMS

There are many reasons why an individual who has been involved in an accident should immediately hire a personal injury attorney. I am a numbers geek, and the numbers show that the average person who hires an attorney is going to recover three times more compensation than the individual who does not retain an attorney. As my mentor and colleague, world-class trial lawyer, William McMurry, told a jury in rural Kentucky in 2004, "It's about the money, folks. Let's be honest here; we have no other way in society and in our legal system to recover damages. Money is what the law allows, so let's be frank here: it is about the money." We do not live in a country that embraces an "eye for an eye" policy of resolving injury claims, so we need to recover monetary damages for our clients that will certainly account for every recoverable element of damages. This is why big insurance companies train their people to act like patron saints to those involved in an injury accident for the initial few days following the accident. They are hedging their bets so as to convince the claimant that she does not need a lawyer and that big insurance will treat her fairly when it comes time to settle her injury claim. They want the claimant to say, "Wow, this company really does what they say they do on TV. They have put me in a rental car and paid me blue book value for my car. So, of course they are going to quickly pay for all of my medical bills, wage loss, and pain and suffering; as well as for my future medical bills and wage losses that are going to arise after I settle the claim with them, right?" Wrong. This is one of big insurance's manipulative tactics that routinely allows them to laugh to themselves while counting their profits at quarterly and annual meetings. If you don't believe me, please go read From Good Hands to Boxing Gloves: The Dark Side of Insurance by David J. Berardinelli for a comprehensive description of one company's shift in claims handling that was made in the 1990s and remains today, allowing for that company to act in complete contradiction to its television advertising statements. The reason the company likely did this? They were keenly aware of the research and data confirming that claimants with attorney representation settled their claims for larger amounts!

DON'T BE A VICTIM OF THE "PITFALL" GAME

As a child, I was addicted to the Atari game "Pitfall." When watching videos of it now, I laugh at how simple the game was in comparison to the graphics, plotlines, and options included in the games my son now plays. In Pitfall, the player (Pitfall Harry) goes through the jungle to recover treasures. The premise was simple: don't fall into a pitfall! If you don't fall into a pitfall, you are able to recover all the treasure. The same is true for personal injury cases: your goal is to be Pitfall Harry, avoid traps, and recover what you are entitled to! Hiring an attorney helps to avoid the pitfalls that often arise during a personal injury case. Too many people try to handle their claim alone, choosing to engage an attorney only if they reach an impasse with the insurance company. Clients who come to me this late in the game are often frustrated by stories of others who came to me earlier with similar facts of the injury accident, yet who recovered much more money. Unfortunately, by waiting that long to consult a professional, claimants often find that they have jeopardized their case by succumbing themselves to insurance pitfalls. By the time these latecomers realize they need an attorney, they have already given a detrimental recorded statement to the insurance company which can be used against them during their personal insurance claim.

Recorded Statements

Recorded statements are one of the most effective ways that insurance companies will trap a claimant. Many people do not realize they are being recorded when they are talking to an insurance company; either state laws do not require the company to tell the individual that the call is being recorded, or the company has trained their personnel to explain the recording rapidly so that it is basically glossed over. The insurance adjuster, who has gone through a million-dollar training program with the billion-dollar big insurance company, has been carefully trained to ask questions that appear very innocent but are actually designed to elicit responses that are going to hurt the claim later in the case. When giving these statements, especially without an attorney's advice, there is no way to undo the potential damage to the case. The claimant's statements are admissible throughout the claims process, and will usually be cited in the context of the litigation if the case is taken to court.

Occasionally, attorneys are hired without having knowledge of a client's prior statements about the case, and the insurance company does not inform the attorneys about these statements. We proceed through such a case, as sworn testimonies are given through depositions and trials, without realizing that the previously recorded statements are being held as a trump card so as to provide impeaching contradiction of what the client is now claiming. Unfortunately, in these situations, there are times when a client is unsure about the facts while giving sworn statements. As attorneys, we advise all of our clients that, if they cannot remember the facts or render an opinion with 100% certainty, they should simply state that they do not remember the answer. We would much rather hear our clients say that they do not remember. This gives them the ability to later amend their statement if they do happen to remember the answer to a question. This same process applies to guessing: it is always better for clients to simply state that they do not remember than to make an "educated" guess about the matter at hand.

Many times, personal injury attorneys are hired after an insurance company has misled the client for several months. Insurance companies report billions of dollars in profits every year. They do not do this by "taking care of" injured victims—paying their lost wages, reimbursing their medical bills, and sending them a substantial check for their pain and suffering. On the contrary, insurance companies post billions of dollars in profits each year by doing precisely the opposite. An insurance adjuster may contact you after an auto accident, agree to pay the fair market value of your vehicle, and promise other financial help that the insurance company never intends to provide. Claimants believe that the insurance company is on their side, especially because of the insurance company advertisements on television with warm voices, compassionate promises to consumers and famous personalities assuring you that you will be treated fairly by this company. In reality, an insurance company is doing everything possible to diminish the value of the claim and encourage a quick settlement, failing to educate the claimant about future damages and the fact that a release will absolve the company from any future claims. In short, insurance companies try to do just enough to keep injured persons from hiring an attorney.

DO NOT TRUST YOUR OWN INSURANCE COMPANY JUST BECAUSE YOU HAVE LOYALLY PAID THEM PREMIUMS FOR YEARS

In cases when an insurance company has to assume financial responsibility to their own insured for an accident, the company has the same incentive to devalue the claim as it would to a third-party claimant. Therefore, even though the insured may have paid premiums and placed his or her trust in this company for any number of years, the insurance company can turn on the insured if they discover that the other person involved in the accident with the insured did not have insurance. In that event, the insurance company is now responsible for paying for the pain and suffering, medical bills, lost wages, and other economic losses of the insured under "Uninsured Motorist" coverage, coverage which carries an extra charge and is required to be provided in several states. Big Insurance will assign insurance adjusters to the claim who are coached, trained, and educated to find ways to devalue the insured's claim.

Attorneys often hear that insurance adjusters called and asked the insured if he or she was feeling well and requested a description of any injuries that he or she may have sustained. In many personal injury cases, the injured person will be feeling okay at the time of the inquiry because latent injuries have not yet manifested symptoms. Insurance adjusters will suggest terms such as "strain" and "sprain" to describe the individual's discomfort, when, in fact, a diagnostic test may reveal that the injured party has sustained a ligament tear or some other structural defect. An insurance company may give the impression that it is going to take care of the claimant's lost wages and medical expenses, without explaining that there is only one opportunity to address all of the damages and that opportunity does not present itself until the end of the claim. By the time the claimant has finally contacted an attorney's office, the financial distress and the damage that has been done are difficult to repair. As attorneys, we are going to do the best that we can. However, it is always best for the clients if they contact our office right after the accident.

The insurance company, whether it is the client's insurance company or the insurance company for the other party, will also send the client paperwork to sign that will include a blanket medical authorization. If this authorization is signed, the insurance company will have the authority to obtain all of the client's medical records from anywhere at any time. The insurance company will tell the client that they need this form to obtain the medical records from the accident. This may be true, but it will also allow them to request medical records from hospitals and primary care physicians prior to the date of the accident. This permits the insurance company to dive deep into the customer's medical history—whether or not it is relevant to the claim at hand—and to potentially use any information that they find to work against the claim. It is frightening to think that with one simple piece of paper, these companies can gain access to documentation that will tell them about the sinus infections you had when you were twelve years old or private personal problems that you've experienced in your twenties or thirties— issues that have nothing whatsoever to do with the accident or the claim in question.

MY $.02 (FREE TO THOSE WHO READ, THOUGH) REGARDING SOME COMMON INQUIRIES

Seek Care Immediately

If you are injured in a traumatic or violent accident, or even if you feel that an accident may have aggravated a pre-existing condition, you should always be seen by a medical professional as soon as possible after the accident. Don't wait to see if the injury will "go away on its own" or if you will be able to "work through it without seeing someone."

The claims of clients who do not seek medical treatment right away and who don't hire an attorney soon after the accident tend to be more difficult to resolve. People that are cautious, seeking medical treatment immediately after an accident and requesting diagnostic tests to determine whether or not they sustained fractures, are much more successful in their claims. Those who do not go to a doctor when they begin feeling pain tend to have more problems proving their claims later on in the case. In most cases, these problems are solvable, but the situation becomes an unnecessary headache.

If It Ain't Broke, Still Fix It!

While emergency rooms carry the latest and greatest technology to determine whether we have broken our bones or have internal bleeding, they typically are not going to perform complex orthopedic and neurological evaluations with MRI scans on an accident victim if fractures and internal bleeding have been ruled out. As such, it is vital that one not simply depend upon the emergency room treatment notes when deciding whether to seek future care. A common insurance company and defense lawyer tactic is to rely upon the emergency room physician's notes (these doctors typically and routinely see 50 patients or more a day and spend less than 10 minutes with each) to devalue a claim, so it is imperative that you seek treatment from qualified (preferably board-certified) specialists for future consultation. As I stated, "If it ain't broke, still fix it!" I cannot count the number of clients I've represented who had traumatic orthopedic and/or neurological injuries that were not discovered at the ER. Don't believe me? Look at the National Football League, who just paid $700 million dollars to settle claims of players who sustained brain injuries which were undetectable on diagnostic testing and which did not result in emergency room care.

Let us consider the NFL concussion litigation and compare it to auto collisions. In NFL concussion cases, the facts surrounded men weighing between 200 and 300 pounds who were hitting each other at less than 10 miles per hour while wearing protective pads and helmets. Furthermore, these men were fully aware that an impact is going to happen. Despite this, these men were still sustaining mild traumatic brain injuries as a result. The NFL, realizing this, is paying more than $700 million dollars to take care of these claims. In an automobile collision, a person may or may not realize that he or she is about to be struck by a vehicle weighing 2,000 to 3,000 pounds and traveling 10–50 miles per hour faster than any NFL player could run. Furthermore, these vehicle occupants lack padding and helmets to protect them upon impact. It makes sense that these collisions cause traumatic brain injuries, whether the injuries are immediately apparent or have long-term effects that may not surface right away.

Show Me the Money (But Only When the Time Is Right)

I went to law school because I wanted to be Jerry Maguire. I wanted to travel the country watching games and dealing with athletes with whom I could develop a family-like bond. So, I chose the law school with a top-notch Sports Law program. Unfortunately, reality struck on day one of law school when the Sports Law Director sadly burst a collective bubble in the room and told all of us that we would not be sports agents and that his program would not benefit us in that regard. Jesus Christ, I had committed to a $150,000 law school education to become the guy who would take down Drew Rosenhaus and Scott Boras and was now being told on day one that this would never happen (but that I was still bound to the tuition pricetag!)? If I couldn't "show the money to athletes," there had to be something else out there. Well, after transferring from this law school to another and reassessing my life's path at least 1,249,202 times, I found it in injury law.

One way that I "show the money" to clients now is through educating them about the proper time to settle claims. While I am not a patient person and do not advocate making victims of injuries waiting unnecessarily for compensation, pitfalls can occur when rushing to settlement. Due to the injuries sustained from an accident, some individuals find themselves out of work and sustaining tremendous financial burdens because of their accident. Bill collectors are calling, and bills are piling up. In these cases, the injured party often makes the mistake of rushing to settlement. Insurance companies can smell this desperation and will jump at the opportunity to come to a quick settlement. They will offer a discounted amount in order to settle the claim right away. Some individuals are desperate for money and will take the settlement for the sake of acquiring the finances they immediately need, rather than patiently waiting for the proper end of the personal injury claim. A quick settlement should never be accepted simply because the individual is feeling better. Rather, the claimant should explore his or her future concerns with the help of both a trusted doctor and attorney, ensuring that those concerns are quantified and given to the insurance company to be included in their evaluation of the claim. Clients must be reminded that there is only one opportunity to settle these claims. They should be reminded that they practiced patience throughout the trauma of the accident and in seeking medical treatment for their injuries; therefore, they should be patient for a few more weeks in order to receive the documentation needed to assure that they receive adequate, full and just compensation for their injuries and sustained damages. Having an established injury attorney to help substantiate the claim and present it to the insurance company will increase the client's chances of a better settlement.

ROAD-MAPPING AN INJURY CLAIM

When clients contact us immediately after an injury, we can give them a "road map" of how the process works. Most clients are surprised when they realize how much paperwork is involved in a personal injury case. Some people have the misconception that personal injury law and personal injury lawyers simply monitor medical treatment and send the insurance company a letter in exchange for a check. However, this process requires much more action than simply requesting copies of medical records and drafting a letter to the insurance company. The attorney must provide the insurance company with evidence to substantiate the claim. If the client waits until the end of the claim to gather the documentation and medical records required to prove said claim, the client will suffer financial hardship for another several months as he or she works to gather the information necessary to reach settlement. Personal injury lawyers, and particularly offices like mine that deal only in personal injury law, recognize that a personal injury claim must be addressed from the very first day with the help of an attorney. Think of this in terms of going to a fine restaurant and trusting the chef to prepare the perfect steak. In this situation, it is important to realize that the chef has more experience in this realm than the customer; thus, the customer should trust the chef.

My firm maintains updated information about the various insurance companies and insurance adjusters who frequently work with us. This helps us to anticipate from the beginning of a case how our client will be treated and how we can capitalize upon that treatment. For example, we know that some insurance companies will intentionally delay claims. In cases involving those insurance companies, our strategy is to keep providing them with more and more information in order to build the value of our client's claim; in this way, the insurance company can act quickly when it is time to reach settlement. In cases of serious injuries, we immediately contact the insurance adjuster and tell him that, while we understand that it may take a little longer to substantiate the seriousness of our client's injuries, we expect for the claim to be resolved in a timely manner, as soon as we are able to quantify the damages and provide the necessary proof to the insurance company. Inevitably, when we treat these insurance companies in this manner, they are taken out of their comfort zone. We are intentionally creating an adversarial situation to ensure that they are on their toes the entire time, and that they know that we will maximize the value of our client's claim in a manner that forces the insurance company to respond adequately.

When discussing personal injury claims, certain questions repeatedly appear. One popular question is, "What if the other driver does not have insurance?" Many people do not know how to handle this situation; they do not receive the proper information from their insurance company when they purchase their policy or when they are reporting a claim. In Kentucky, insurance companies are required to offer drivers "Mandatory Uninsured Motorist Coverage" (UM) as part of their automobile insurance policy. If the driver chooses not to carry this coverage, the insurance company must obtain the rejection in writing and file it with the State of Kentucky. This indicates how important the state feels it is for every driver to carry UM coverage. UM coverage protects drivers in the event that they are involved in an accident with an uninsured motorist. This coverage is offered in increments, with the minimum amount being $25,000 in Kentucky. To my knowledge, there is no maximum. UM coverage has very inexpensive premiums and is easily one of the best bargains that a driver will find for the protection it offers. No one wants to be involved in a serious accident that results in permanent traumatic injuries through no fault of their own only to find that the person who changed his or her life forever has no insurance coverage. However, if such an unfortunate event were to occur, the driver would be protected, as long as UM coverage is part of his or her automobile insurance policy. This coverage continues to follow the driver everywhere. For example, if a customer of UM coverage is riding in a friend's automobile when it becomes involved in an accident with a driver who has no insurance, the UM coverage will step in to help. Furthermore, in Kentucky, stackable coverage is available. Therefore, yours and your friend's UM coverage will apply to the situation. You can actually "stack" both policies' coverage on top of each other in order to create more coverage. Many people without an attorney do not realize that they have this option, and the insurance company often does not explain this information voluntarily, even if UM coverage is included in the insurance package.

Another question that attorneys often hear is, "I have been injured in an accident, and I have medical bills as a result of the accident. Who is going to pay them?" Common sense would dictate that the driver who caused the accident should be responsible for paying the injured party's medical expenses. However, Kentucky is a no-fault state; therefore, if you have your own automobile insurance policy, you will have $10,000 in coverage to pay for medical expenses or lost wages. Medical coverage is separate and has nothing to do with Uninsured Motorist Coverage or Underinsured Motorist Coverage. In this state, a driver does not need to have full coverage in order to have medical no-fault coverage or personal injury coverage to pay for medical expenses or lost wages. Furthermore, Kentucky provides the right to reserve the benefits and direct payment of benefits. This ensures that the entire $10,000 will not be paid to the first medical provider that bills clients for services. It allows clients to direct a portion of the money to pay for their lost wages and reserve some of the funds for future medical bills. This becomes important when specialists require a guarantee that they will be paid before they will see the patient or perform diagnostic tests. We can use the medical no-fault coverage to provide assurance to these medical providers, so that our clients receive the medical treatment and prescriptions that they need to recover. Once the injured party exceeds the $10,000 medical no-fault coverage, a claim can be made against the other driver's insurance for the rest of the medical bills. On the other hand, if you are involved in an accident and the other driver is at fault but you do not have automobile insurance, you may be penalized by the State of Kentucky and not permitted to collect the first $10,000 in medical no-fault coverage. This fact underscores how important Kentucky has made it, from a public policy perspective, for people to carry their own automobile insurance coverage.

"What if I want to sue? What if we want to take this to court?" This is a frequent question that personal injury attorneys hear. Now is an excellent time to mention that personal injury attorneys are not right off the set of Law & Order or Perry Mason; we do not simply file a personal injury lawsuit and take the case before a jury the following week. Because it is such a lengthy process to arrive at a jury trial in Kentucky, most of our personal injury cases settle out of court here. However, we do have a jury system that allows us to litigate claims and take cases to a jury trial, if warranted. We discuss these situations with our clients at great length, and many are reassured when they realize that we are not like Law & Order; their cases will probably settle prior to a jury trial. Our clients do want justice, and some feel as if their insurance company is bullying them. We are not a law firm that allows our clients to be pushed around by an insurance company, and we never advise any of our clients to accept a low-ball settlement offer just to avoid going to court. Yes, going to court in Kentucky is a fairly expensive and lengthy process. But with that said, it is important to understand that we, as a law firm, incur this cost, as well as all other case expenses, and that we work under a contingency fee basis. In short, we accept all of the risk of taking the case to trial. If we are successful, then we will be paid. If we are unsuccessful, we will not inflict those losses on the client. This allows some people, who would otherwise be unable to do so, to have the necessary freedom to embrace the jury and the litigation process.

As clients are trying to decide if they should hire our firm, they will often ask, "How do I pick a personal injury attorney and law firm? How do I know who is the right choice for me?" What clients may not realize about our law firm is that we screen them just as thoroughly as they screen us. We like to find clients that are a good match for the work that we strive to do and that fit our model. We are not very patient people; we like to move these claims and keep the insurance companies on their toes. We want to make sure that our clients are individuals who can deal with our constant requests to perform investigative work and keep us informed about medical care, so that we can keep the insurance companies informed as well. We want a system in which insurance adjusters have to set reserves for our claims. Insurance companies set aside what they think would be the top-dollar offer for the claim. If they are not updated with constant information about the claim, they will not be prepared for a demand letter for tens or hundreds of thousands of dollars in excess of what they have put aside to pay the claim. However, if the personal injury attorney is doing his or her job correctly, the insurance company will be constantly updated about the client's medical condition. In this case, when the demand letter is sent, stating what is expected as compensation for the client, the insurance company is not overly surprised, because they have been constantly increasing the reserve based on the information the attorney has been providing them. We depend on our clients to give us information that we can disseminate to the insurance company. However, if our client is going to become annoyed when we contact them every couple of weeks, then we are probably not a good fit for them. Typically, we find that our clients appreciate the constant contact. If they do not, there are certainly other firms available that will try to settle the case for a generic sum that is associated with the type of claim that the client has, but that is not the way our firm operates.

As identified previously, my best mentor has been William "Bill" McMurry. I have had the privilege of working with him for a couple of years, and he is certainly a rock star among trial attorneys who, in my opinion, would be on a Mt. Rushmore of trial lawyers in Kentucky. He constantly preaches the importance of diligence, focus, and preparation when handling a personal injury case. He specifically maintains a smaller caseload so that he can master every minor detail of each case, just as though he were taking it before a jury and asking for an award of millions of dollars. I think this holds true for all of those in my profession: we must treat each case like the personal, individual case that it is, rather than just another "file folder." We must meet with our clients, get to know them and their families, and develop a relationship with them. We must develop a camaraderie with them that will encourage us to maximize the clients' interests and truly respect their trust in us. We must identify experts early and often and choose them specific to the case and client.

Only when one gets to this point as a personal injury attorney will she truly be the best advocate for her clients. If she simply makes a few telephone calls to an insurance company and speaks about her client as if this is just another claim, the insurance company will win. It is her job, as the attorney, to humanize the claim and to deal with it as though it is unlike any other claim she has ever dealt with before. That is the only way to deal with a case, because, let's face it, everyone has his or her own set of problems. Everybody has personal situations to deal with, and it is our job as attorneys to recognize those issues, to pinpoint them, and to accurately demonstrate them to the insurance company. We must do this in order to make the insurance company understand that if they do not take the claim seriously and treat this person as an individual rather than a claim number, they will certainly be exposed in litigation, and they will lose the trial.

At this time, I would like to address automobile accidents, because there are multiple components to those types of claims that people may not realize exist. There are many situations in which individuals could encounter pitfalls if they are not experienced in handling personal injury claims. For example, in automobile accident cases, there are certain actions that must be taken, especially here in Kentucky. If a person is involved in an automobile accident, he or she should always call 911 to report the accident. Calls to 911 are recorded, and the caller can obtain a written transcript of the call to substantiate to the insurance company what he or she said. It is also possible to find independent witnesses by reviewing the 911 transcripts. Motorists that witnessed the accident and called 911 without stopping at the scene of the accident will be noted on the 911 transcripts. These independent witnesses can substantiate how the accident happened in order to establish fault and provide testimony about the nature of the impact and whether or not it was an impact that could have caused injuries.

You should always request that the police respond to the scene of the accident. That way, the responding officer can provide written documentation about the details of the accident, verify the other driver's information and insurance, and issue citations to the other driver, citing human factors that were the approximate cause of the accident. As attorneys, we frequently see individuals who try to be good Samaritans, trusting the other driver's suggestion that the parties simply exchange information and allow their respective insurance companies to work out paying the repair costs. Unfortunately, there are several too-common outcomes to these situations. Often, the other driver produces an insurance card that, unbeknownst to the injured party, has been canceled. In other cases, the other driver claims responsibility at the accident, but denies this later when speaking to the insurance company. Some people blatantly lie about what happened and produce "witnesses" to verify their false version of how the accident occurred. These witnesses will state that it is impossible that the injured party could have suffered to the extent being claimed. Having the police respond to the accident is not the same as having an advocate on the claimant's side; it is simply the best way to introduce an impartial third party to the scene and reduce all of the information to writing, which can then be used in an individual's personal injury claim.

One thing that should be explored right away is the possibility of a liability concern. Kentucky is a comparative fault state, which makes automobile accidents easier for Kentuckians to face. When evaluating a claim, it must be determined what percentage of fault may be placed upon the parties involved in the accident. In some states, if you are even 1% at fault, you are barred from recovery damages from the other party. However, in Kentucky, you can actually be up to 99% at fault for an accident and still recover for the 1% that was not your fault.

This enables attorneys to find extenuating circumstances that may have contributed to the accident. For example, we will try to discover if the other driver was using a cell phone at the time of the accident. The insurance company will not voluntarily give us this information, but we do put them on notice to have their insured preserve his or her cell phone records. That way, if we must go to trial, we can get these records quickly in order to determine whether or not the cell phone was in use at the time of the accident. Other factors that could be attributable to an accident include the use of alcohol or prescription medication, vehicle maintenance issues such as faulty brakes, or distractions within the vehicle itself. This is one reason that it is important to obtain police reports; any indication of the presence of one or more of these elements must be discovered. As attorneys in Kentucky, we have the ability to pull complete criminal background checks upon all residents of the state. We take full advantage of this by running a criminal history of the parties in an accident to determine whether they have a history of similar behavior, or even a criminal propensity.

One element that we are seeing more often in automobile accident claims is the use of social media. Often, we are able to obtain helpful information contained on a defendant's social media site, and we have found that some people post information about the accident, making statements such as, "I was at this crazy party and then I was in an accident an hour later." This is information we want to obtain early in the case. We can then give it to the insurance company and prove to them that there were situations surrounding this accident that may place part, if not all, of the liability upon the defendant. Social media is a valuable tool in helping to discover the skeletons in the defendant's closet.

In the same way, our own clients' use of social media is important. A client can harm his or her claim simply by posting something on a social media page (i.e., Facebook, Twitter, LinkedIn, etc.) that reflects poorly upon his or her character. It does not need to be specific to the accident in order to harm his or her case. Anything that reveals that the client tends toward certain bad habits or would not present well could hurt the case. These multi-billion dollar insurance companies have investigators who discover these flaws and keep the information in their back pockets, ready to throw at the injured party when he or she tries to make a large claim. This is a very important topic that we try to discuss with our clients at the very beginning of their cases.

Another element to be dealt with in automobile accidents is the mechanism of injury. For example, a client may try to claim a traumatic brain injury, but if there is only one small dent on the bumper of his or her car and the police report states that the cars were traveling about one mile per hour at the time of the accident, the claim is going to be very difficult. I have had clients who flipped a vehicle three times and walked away with a little bit of whiplash, and we have settled their claims in less than two months. On the other hand, I have had clients who have experienced less than $500 in property damage, but the clients themselves had sustained life-changing injuries. In these cases, it is imperative for attorneys to hire people who can examine the evidence and explain why this occurred. At times, we have had to hire biomechanical engineers to discuss the mechanism of injury and how certain accidents can cause certain injuries to occur. There are also accident re-constructionists who can recreate the accident scene in order to decipher how the accident happened, record the data from the vehicles involved, and produce a report that explains to a lay person what happened and why. We engage these experts regularly and rely upon them to find the truth, especially in cases of serious injuries that could either be deemed questionable, or that deal directly with a question of liability.

In Kentucky, there is one particular rule that often surprises people. If the driver of a car hits you on purpose—such as in the case of road rage—you can make a claim against his or her insurance company, but you are limited as to the amount you are able to recover. If someone purposely hits you, you may only recover up to $25,000—the state's minimum coverage—from his or her insurance company. However, having $25,000 at your disposal to resolve a claim in an intentional accident is an improvement on the laws of some states, in which you would receive no financial help at all.

The "collateral source rule" prohibits juries from hearing evidence explaining that an insurance company is covering the claims. Plaintiff attorneys sometimes despise this rule, as we do not want juries assuming that the defendant, who may be an indigent or impoverished person, will be required to pay the judgment out of his or her own pocket. Even though everyone but the jury knows that there is an insurance company involved, none of us can bring this up during the trial. However, this sometimes works to our advantage in cases when a family member is at fault. In some automobile accident cases, we see children or other loved ones suffering traumatic injuries when their parent or family member is the driver at fault. In most of those cases, the insurance company settles prior to the case going to court, because the family member who is at fault is remorseful and will not deny any responsibility. At times, the driver will express remorse to the jury and may even beg the jury to make sure that the victim is compensated. If the jury knew that the family member, who is testifying that he or she is remorseful and completely at fault, is not going to pay the judgment, then the jury may award a larger claim. This is a case in which the collateral source rule works to our advantage.

Another type of personal injury case that our law firm handles is motorcycle accidents. These types of accidents tend to be the most frightening situations and often result in the most serious injuries. It only takes a split second for a motorcycle accident to occur. These accidents are often caused by drivers who are talking and texting on their cell phones; these careless drivers are becoming an increasing problem in our society. Motorcycle accidents are also typically found in cases of road rage, other forms of distraction, or simply as a result of the motorist looking away from the road for a second. It is difficult enough to see these smaller vehicles during the day, but the situation worsens at night, when all that can be seen is one small headlight coming through the darkness. We strongly encourage clients who have been involved in motorcycle accidents to reconsider their passions and their hobbies. If they must ride motorcycles, we are strong advocates for the use of helmets.

In these cases, we are dealing with individuals who have been violently thrown into the air and who, regardless of whether or not they were wearing a helmet, have generally suffered some type of trauma to the head and orthopedic limbs. In these situations, a brain injury assessment is necessary to determine if there are signs of anything from a mild to a moderate traumatic brain injury, such as changes in personality, loss of consciousness, or a prolonged dazed state. In consideration of the increasing number of concussion litigation cases and how they occur, the chance that a brain injury may have been suffered should be taken seriously. Unfortunately, in Kentucky, most motorcycle drivers purchase only the state's minimum requirements for insurance, as that is the least expensive option. However, because motorcycle accidents tend to be very traumatic and injurious, there is often not enough insurance to cover the amount of damage sustained. We recommend to our clients that they purchase the maximum amount of coverage, in addition to purchasing Uninsured and Underinsured Motorist Coverage, even though the last two types of coverage mentioned are not required for motorcycles in Kentucky. It is frightening to think of motorcyclists traveling down the highway with so many "weapons" coming at them, perhaps operated by people who are intoxicated or not paying attention to the road, and it is still more frightening to think that these bikers are driving without sufficient insurance to protect them in the event of an accident.

A trucking accident case differs greatly from an automobile accident case or a motorcycle accident case. There is an entire laundry list of things that must be done immediately following a trucking accident. Any attorney that is retained in one of these cases should immediately do his or her due diligence to ensure that evidence is preserved and that everything is done correctly and quickly to protect his or her client's interests. Otherwise, the client may not receive a fair and just compensation for the injuries sustained.

Truck accident claims involve complex federal regulations and evidence that must be preserved to ensure a successful claim. Therefore, it is imperative that a personal injury attorney is hired as quickly as possible following the accident. Some truck drivers are being abused by their employers and forced to drive more hours than they are legally permitted. These drivers are not completing their daily logs or performing daily maintenance on their trucks, and they are falling asleep at the wheel. In short, some truck drivers are driving their 30,000-pound "weapons" while they are distracted. If you are injured as the result of a driver's negligence, you are entitled to all of the information available about the cause of the accident itself, and how it could have been prevented from the perspective of both the driver and the driver's employer.

In addition to preserving evidence, the injured party is also faced with complex and convoluted insurance policies that are difficult to interpret, unless you have experience in the trucking industry or in truck accident trials. For example, one insurance company may cover the driver while he is working, and another company may cover him when he is operating the vehicle during his off-duty hours. There may even be a third insurer that covers the cargo that is in the trailer and a fourth that covers the trailer without the tractor. If you are suffering traumatic injuries and do not know how to navigate the various insurance providers for the truck, you may not be fully compensated. The trucking company will not voluntarily inform you of the various policies that exist. Trucking companies are notorious for extreme aggression after accidents because they know their exposure in regard to claims. We have a previous trucking adjuster working with us who has told us countless stories of how the trucking company would send him to hospitals all over the country almost daily, check in hand, to compensate the families of an injured person. The notion of someone who is heavily sedated, in the hospital, being coerced into settling a claim, and accepting a check without knowing his future medical condition is frightening indeed.

Insurance companies for truckers are difficult to deal with. However, so are the truckers themselves. A trucker's most valuable commodity is his commercial driver's license or CDL. A commercial driver's license is subject to revocation or suspension if the trucker is involved in an accident. Therefore, truckers have incentive to lie or manipulate the fact patterns associated with the accident, because to lose their CDL is to lose their livelihood. However, equipped on that truck is usually enough information to contradict what the driver is saying, if you only know how to get that information. When you do get this information and you find that the trucker is lying, it generally leads to a greater resolution for the case. As personal injury attorneys, we are very enthusiastic about cases like that. If a trucking accident case is not handled correctly, it could expose the victim to having his claim denied, failing to have his claim maximized, or having his claim covered by a smaller amount of insurance than is actually available.

Now, let us discuss accidents that happen outside of the vehicle: namely, pedestrian accident claims. These types of claims are generally found in higher-volume areas, particularly in school districts and places known for heavy traffic. In Kentucky, we have many pedestrian accidents in large cities, such as Louisville; our smaller counties do not see as many of these accidents. Unfortunately, many people do not understand the laws regarding the pedestrians' right-of-way. Pedestrian accidents are a huge catalyst for brain injuries, because the victim's head very often strikes the vehicle and then the pavement. Many of these claims involve children. As attorneys, we take pedestrian accidents very seriously, due to the nature of and propensity for serious injuries. This is particularly true in the case of injuries to children and minors that, unfortunately, may linger with them forever.

In Kentucky, if you are a pedestrian who is involved in an accident with a vehicle, the insurance policy covering that vehicle will be the source of two claims. It will be the source of the liability claim to pay for your damages because of your injuries, pain, and suffering; and it will also pay for your excess medical expenses. Your personal injury protection carrier can also contribute toward medical expenses through your $10,000 no-fault coverage. Your own coverage can stack on top of this coverage so, once again, if you have Underinsured Motorist Coverage or if you live with somebody who does, you should make sure that you have an attorney file those claims quickly. One element we have not discussed is Underinsured Motorist Coverage. Like UM coverage, this is an extra policy that you purchase with your automobile insurance which covers you in the event that the at-fault party does not have sufficient insurance to cover all of your damages. In Kentucky, there are certain processes and protocols that must be followed in order for you to be eligible to make a claim under your Underinsured Motorist Coverage. If you do not follow the processes correctly, the consequences can include losing your right to that coverage.

When litigating claims in pedestrian cases, there are several factors that must be taken under consideration. First, it is important to realize that a pedestrian is not necessarily at fault simply because he or she was not in the crosswalk at the moment of impact. In these cases, it is important to consider the oncoming driver who hit the individual. Did the driver have ample opportunity to avoid the accident? Was he or she engaged in distracting behavior? What was the visibility like on that day? These questions must be carefully reviewed when litigating claims in these cases. Another element that an attorney should review is the post-impact conduct of the defendant. If the driver simply sits in his or her car, calls 911, and does not get out to check on the pedestrian or express any remorse, we will expose this information in front of a jury. On the other hand, if the driver rushes out of his or her car, tries to call for help, and recruits EMS to come assist the pedestrian as soon as possible, then it will be more difficult for the pedestrian to win the case. Of course, we like to think, and we certainly hope, that there are good Samaritans in the world, but frequently, there are not. It is disturbing to see the number of people who will cause accidents, then sit in their cars waiting for the police to show up rather than checking on the injured party. Some drivers even scream and yell about how their day has been ruined, despite the fact that their own inattention caused someone else to be injured.

Aside from accidents involving vehicles, my firm often handles premises liability claims. This is a broad term, at least in the scope and context of our office. We include a few different types of cases within the premises liability category; one of these is a general slip-and-fall that may occur at a big box retailer, such as Wal-Mart or Kroger. Premises liability also covers situations such as food poisoning or finding a foreign object in your food at a restaurant. At our law firm, premises liability entails any situation in which you can hold a third party responsible for an injury that occurred while you were on their premises. Often, we must conduct a meticulous analysis of the claim, because the vast majority of these types of claims will be filed against a big box retailer or other type of large retail company. In those cases, since most retailers are self-insured, we are actually dealing with a claims management company, rather than an insurance company. Wal-Mart is so big, the owners have created their own claims management company in order to adjust and investigate their premises liability claims. When you settle the claim, it is Wal-Mart itself, not an insurance company, which pays the claim. In these types of cases, you must be thorough, methodical, and aggressive. I once had a colleague tell me, "When you're going after somebody's own pocketbook, it's much tougher than going after an insurance company."

The analogy that this colleague gave was that of a child who approaches his grandfather to ask for money in order to go to the movies. The grandfather does not pull out a $100 bill and give it to his grandchild, saying, "Have a great time." Rather, he pulls out a dollar at a time, and his stress seems to grow as he gives his grandchild the second dollar, then the third dollar. By the time he has given his grandchild the money for the entire ticket price, he looks as though he has just given the boy his entire retirement account. This story is a wonderful example of what happens when we encounter these retailers and self-insured entities. They are not under the same obligations as insurance companies are—to act fairly and in good faith when negotiating settlement. It is not possible to claim allegations of bad faith under the insurance code when dealing with these companies. Instead, the injured party must do a superb job of proving his or her claim and hope that the company will take the claim seriously and keep it out of court.

If they do not take the claim seriously, then we proceed to litigate the claim against these companies. We have found that we have a slight advantage when we proceed to litigate a premises liability claim. Because these companies do not have an insurance company to pay for the defense of claims (including attorney fees), the average claim value increases quite a bit as the company begins to perform a cost analysis. The company does not like the idea of paying a defense attorney somewhere between $150 to $400 an hour, when they know that my firm is going to do whatever it can to run up those billable hours quickly and force them to defend the claim vigorously. This strategy tends to work very well for us. With that being said, there are certainly situations in which we must carefully consider whether or not we should take our premises liability to court. Sometimes, we want to see if the retailer will produce a copy of the surveillance videotape of the accident in the pre-litigation period. This can be considered either work product, or an item that does not have to be produced without a discovery request. We try to help the retailer understand that, if they have video footage that is favorable to them and that they do not want to share with us, they will inevitably have to turn it over to us in court. In the meantime, the retailer is spending a lot of money adjusting the claim or hiring defense attorneys, when simply releasing the footage to us could have cleared up the entire matter.

In premises liability cases, it is imperative to inform the retailers immediately of the potential of litigation. This process is called "a demand for preservation of evidence." With this demand, we are requesting that they preserve anything and everything that could allow us to investigate this claim, if it goes to court. The reason that we love to employ this tactic is that, if the retailer disregards our request and does not preserve the evidence, they are guilty of exfoliation of evidence. If we get to trial and find that a video of the incident is missing or an employee incident report has been lost, I instruct that the jury may infer that the lost information would have been unfavorable to the case of the retailer. Therefore, it is extremely important to put the retailer on notice to preserve all of the evidence because, inevitably, there are times when the evidence is lost, and it may be the advantage that the client needs to win the case against the retailer.

In a premises liability case, there is always the possibility that the client should have seen the danger on the premises. In this case, it is our client's fault that he or she was injured. Thankfully, the Supreme Court abolished the "open and obvious" doctrine last year. Now, insurance companies are unable to simply declare and win a case against the injured party without appearing before a jury. However, if the client falls into a five-by-ten-foot puddle of pink Kool-Aid, it is very likely that the jury will say that the client should have seen the puddle and thus cannot recover the claim. While these cases are undeniably challenging, the firm cannot help but find them enjoyable.

The profession of a personal injury attorney is one that requires focus and humility. Attorneys who allow their egos to consume them cannot empathize with their client, their client's concerns, or what their client is dealing with as a result of his or her injury. We must embrace the task of placing our client's needs before our financial desires, remaining focused and dedicated to the case from the very beginning. When we do this, the cards will stack in our favor, and all of our clients will receive the best possible representation.

(This content should be used for informational purposes only. It does not create an attorney-client relationship with any reader and should not be construed as legal advice. If you need legal advice, please contact an attorney in your community who can assess the specifics of your situation.)

3

DO YOU NEED A PERSONAL INJURY ATTORNEY?

by Janet Ward Black, Esq.

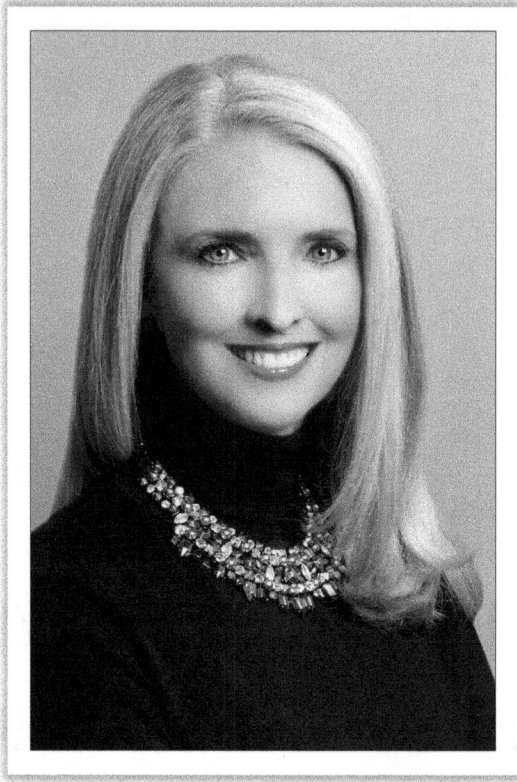

Janet Ward Black, Esq.
Ward Black Law
Greensboro, North Carolina

Janet Ward Black owns Ward Black Law, one of North Carolina's largest woman-owned law firms.

A graduate of Davidson College and Duke Law School, Black served as president of the North Carolina Academy of Trial Lawyers and president of the North Carolina Bar Association. She is only the second lawyer in North Carolina history to serve as president of both organizations.

The program she created while president of the NCBA, "4 ALL," has been used as a model in the US and Canada for providing free legal services to the poor.

She and her firm have been named in Best Lawyers in America and Best Law Firms in America.

DO YOU NEED A PERSONAL INJURY ATTORNEY?

So you've been hurt and it was someone else's fault. Do you need an attorney?

When deciding whether to hire a personal injury attorney, you must first determine the severity of your injuries and the amount of damages sustained as a result of those injuries. Many people automatically assume that they need to hire an attorney when they are involved in an accident or suffer an injury that is someone else's fault. This is not always true!

If the injuries are modest, such as in a car accident requiring a single trip to the emergency room and no follow-up with a physician, the damages are probably relatively small. Most personal injury attorneys are paid a contingency fee for their work. That means that the attorney is paid a percentage of the amount they recover for their client. It may be difficult, therefore, to find a personal injury attorney willing to take a case with modest damages. Alternatively, paying an attorney by the hour to handle such a small case could end up costing the injured person more than her case is worth! In this scenario, the injured person is likely to be best served by settling their claim with the insurance company on their own and not retaining a personal injury attorney. So what should you do next?

THE INSURANCE ADJUSTER IS NOT YOUR FRIEND!

The risk of not having attorney representation in a personal injury case is that you may be lulled into a false sense of trust with other parties involved in the case. For example, the adjusters representing the at-fault party's insurance company may tell you that they honestly want to help; that they want to be "fair" and do only what is best for all parties, including you. However, in many states, including North Carolina, insurance adjusters have no obligation to tell injured persons that their job is to settle claims by paying as little as they can and, that they are not required to deal fairly with you.

If the insurance adjuster is allowed to build trust with the injured person, they may develop an unfair advantage. The insurance adjuster can use this unfair advantage as they discharge their professional obligation to their employer to settle the claim for less than the claim is worth. Claimants may even be lulled into making decisions about settlement without all of the relevant information or even understanding what information they need in order to make an informed decision.

An individual involved in an accident with substantial medical expenses or long-term consequences (such as a permanent disability or injuries requiring surgery) should always have a personal injury attorney representing their interests. The attorney is educated in the laws of the state, knows if the insurance adjusters are being truthful, and knows how to deal with insurance companies and their attorneys.

One example of why the seriously injured person needs an attorney who understands the law is a recent North Carolina statute called "Billed vs. Paid." Under this statute, an injured party is allowed to collect only the amount for medical bills that were actually paid to medical providers. If you sustain an injury and are treated in an emergency room, the charge could be $400, but your health insurance company may have an agreement with the hospital that allows it to pay a reduced amount of $200 on the $400 bill. A reasonable person might think that they can recover the full $400 from the other person's insurance company, but that is not the case! You are entitled to recover only $200 – the amount actually paid by your health insurance company - and you may have to repay that $200 to your health insurance provider. As a result, you receive no compensation for the medical bill, even though you paid your health insurance premiums. Many layers of complexity are involved in personal injury cases; the more severe the injury, the more complex the case becomes. Having an attorney who understands the law and has experience in personal injury cases can help you recover all of the damages to which you are entitled.

The first step in hiring a personal injury attorney is finding an attorney that you trust. We are called "Attorneys and Counselors at Law," meaning that we are obligated to give clients our best advice, sharing our wisdom, knowledge, and experience to help them make the best decision. As attorneys, we must help our clients decide whether to settle for a particular amount or take the case to trial. Therefore, you need to feel confident that you can trust your attorney's judgment and expertise in the area of personal injury law.

The second step is to find a personal injury attorney who understands, and has experience in, every step of the litigation process, because no two personal injury cases are alike and they can quickly become very complex. Let me walk you through a case to give you a better idea of the complexities that can be involved in a personal injury case.

WHAT ARE THE STEPS INVOLVED?

A twenty year old girl (let's call her Jane) is coming home from church. She is driving in her lane of traffic at the prescribed speed limit and she is not distracted in any way by the use of a cell phone or other device. A tractor-trailer jackknifes, crosses three lanes of traffic, and lands on top of Jane's car with one of the wheels striking her head and crushing her shoulder. Jane's shoulder injury is catastrophic. The first thing that a personal injury attorney must do is try to determine who is "at fault," that is, who is responsible for causing this accident.

The first step is to research and gather information about the driver, the owner, and the insurer of the tractor-trailer. The reliability of the drivers' accounts of the wreck must be evaluated and other information about the parties involved in the accident must be developed. Personal injury attorneys work with police officers to obtain the information gathered at the accident scene: photographs, documentation of skid marks, witness statements, etc. The attorneys interview witnesses who may have seen the accident, which may add more detail that might not have been provided in the official accident report. All of this is undertaken to determine if the tractor-trailer driver did something wrong to cause the accident or if the accident was unavoidable.

The next step is to evaluate the injuries sustained in the accident. In this case, Jane had four very serious shoulder surgeries that resulted in medical bills of over $100,000. Unfortunately, Jane's condition did not improve and she continued to experience terrible headaches for more than a year after the accident. When Jane initially complained of ongoing head-aches, the doctors were more concerned with her shoulder injury. They attributed her headaches and inability to focus on the pain medicines she was taking, her various shoulder surgeries, and the effects of her extensive recovery process.

Jane's attorney was not satisfied with the doctors brushing aside her complaints about headaches, so she kept pushing her doctors to take her complaints seriously. Jane was sent by her attorney to a series of neurologists who determined that she had also suffered a severe head injury during the accident. Before the tire and wheel hit Jane's shoulder, it hit her head, causing a very complicated brain injury that left her IQ intact but impaired her ability to process complex thoughts. Sadly, this injury made it impossible for Jane to work in her chosen field. Her head injury was not obvious to Jane or her medical professionals for more than a year after the accident because the symptoms were masked by her shoulder injuries.

Once her attorney had a clear understanding of who was at fault and of Jane's injuries, the settlement negotiation process began with the insurance company for the driver and the tractor-trailer owner. To negotiate the best possible settlement for Jane, her attorney had to convince the insurance company of the severity of Jane's injuries, that those injuries were caused as a direct result of the truck driver's actions and inactions, and that no one was at fault other than the driver of the tractor-trailer. Finally, Jane's attorneys had to be absolutely clear that, if the case did not settle for a reasonable sum and had to go to a trial, Jane and her attorneys would be able to convince a jury of the immense permanent impact of the driver's negligence on Jane's life.

A settlement was successfully negotiated with the truckers' insurance carrier and Jane was able to recover damages in an amount that was fair. At that point, additional negotiations began with Jane's own medical insurance provider and any doctors or hospitals, that had not yet been paid in full. The attorneys worked very hard to ensure that Jane received as much of the settlement proceeds as possible, rather than having those funds used to pay medical expenses or to reimburse the health insurance companies that paid for Jane's treatment. These were just a few of the challenges and obstacles that arose during Jane's case and they demonstrate how an injured party can greatly benefit from involving an experienced personal injury attorney in a complex case.

EXPERIENCE MATTERS. (AND SO DOES WHETHER THE LAWYER WILL RETURN YOUR PHONE CALLS OR NOT!)

Let me explain a little more about why an injured person should retain a personal injury attorney, rather than a general practice attorney who handles many different types of cases, for representation in a complicated injury case. Even though all lawyers have gone to law school, that does not mean that each one has experience or knowledge in the same areas of law. In this way, attorneys are much like physicians; you would not go to a foot doctor if you needed brain surgery. When you are injured, you want an attorney who specializes in injury law and who has a proven track record of success in handling complex personal injury cases. In addition to hiring an attorney who has a tremendous amount of experience in personal injury law, you want an attorney who will listen to you. This willingness to listen applies not just to the attorney, but extends to the attorney's staff, legal assistants, and paralegals assigned to your case. You should feel confident that your attorney and their staff will keep you informed as to the progress of your case and that you will be able to get answers to all of your questions as the case progresses.

Some of the most common complaints that are made about attorneys include: "I never hear from my lawyer," "I don't know what is going on in my case," and "I don't know if they are doing a good job." It may be that your attorney is doing a good job and that they are working aggressively on your case, but they simply have not taken the time to contact you to convey what actions they have taken on your behalf or when you can expect your case to settle. However, it is important for you to know these things because it is your case! You want an attorney who is willing to talk to you about your case regularly or have a staff member who will do so whenever you have a question or want to check on the status. Sometimes clients think their case will be resolved very quickly when, in reality, it may take a very long time to settle a personal injury case or to take the case to trial. It is important for you to be able to talk to your attorney or his staff when you have a question or a concern about your case. Always look for a lawyer who will make a commitment to keeping you informed of the progress of your case.

DON'T SETTLE TOO SOON!

The fact is that you do not want to rush through your personal injury case, especially if you have a severe injury. Rushing to settle quickly may mean that you settle for less money than you should! You have only one opportunity to recover damages for the injuries the other person caused. You want to make certain, therefore, that you have been examined and treated by all of the necessary doctors and specialists to recover your health to the maximum extent possible.

For example, let's say that you are involved in an automobile accident, and the insurance company offers you a quick settlement, which is something insurance companies often do. You agree to the terms offered, even though your back is still hurting, because you have a lot of medical bills, you haven't been able to work because of your injuries, and money has become very tight. This settlement agreement releases the insurance company and the at-fault party from any further responsibility for your injuries. But a few months after signing the release, you discover that you actually sustained a ruptured disc in the accident and that surgery is required. Because you signed the release, however, you cannot go back to the insurance company for more money for the surgery. You should move very deliberately through your personal injury case to make certain that all of your damages, injuries, and expenses are understood and well-documented. You should see all of the necessary medical providers to ensure that all of your injuries have been discovered and treated. Also, if you still are not fully recovered when you finish treatment, ask your health care provider if there is anything more you can do to return to normal. If not, your doctor may assign you a "disability rating." A disability rating is important when your attorney is negotiating your case because it quantifies any temporary or permanent effects of your injuries and can help persuade the insurance adjuster that your case is strong and your attorney is thorough. Often, it is in the best interests of the insurance company to settle your claim rather than to risk going to trial and having a jury return a verdict for a larger amount.

So I Might Have To Pay My Health Insurance Company Back?

Some of you may be wondering about my earlier reference to the "right of reimbursement" with regard to health insurance companies, including Medicare, Medicaid, or other insurers that have paid medical bills on behalf of an injured person. Let me elaborate with another example. A 66-year-old man is involved in an automobile accident and is transported to the hospital. He is admitted and remains in the hospital for a week while being treated for his injuries. All of his medical bills during his hospital stay, as well as his subsequent follow-ups with physicians are paid by Medicare. In most instances, if you are a Medicare beneficiary and your injuries were sustained as a result of the fault of another, any proceeds that you recover from the at-fault party must be used to reimburse Medicare for the medical expenses it paid on your behalf. If you do not reimburse Medicare from your settlement proceeds, Medicare can halt future benefits and payments until you reimburse Medicare in full for the payments it made for your accident injuries.

In my experience, many individuals who try to settle their own personal injury claims do not realize that Medicare, Medicaid, and even some private health insurers can deny future benefits and payments, or even sue you, if you don't reimburse them for medical bills they paid on your behalf once you have settled. For example, individuals may assume they can just keep all of a $3,000 settlement they receive after being injured, not realizing there may be repercussions, until they receive demands for payment from the government or their health insurance company. This is another risk of trying to settle a personal injury claim without the advice and counsel of an experienced personal injury attorney. There is no opportunity for a "free lunch" or a double recovery. If your health insurance provider has paid your medical expenses and you recover a settlement from the at-fault party, you may be required to reimburse your health insurance provider under some circumstances.

WATCH FOR LANDMINES

Let me next review some "landmines" that can undermine a personal injury case. Many people want to believe that the person they are talking to won't take advantage of them. However, in an adversarial situation, such as an automobile accident, statements that you make to an insurance adjuster can (and will, if they are helpful to the insurance company) be used against you. For example, assume that someone hits your car and it is clearly his fault, but he is seriously injured. It is only human nature to rush to his side to inquire if he is okay and say something like: "I am sorry! Are you okay?" That one phrase, "I am sorry," can be interpreted to mean that you are accepting responsibility for the accident that the other driver actually caused. You must be very careful that you do not make any statements that can be construed against you to damage your case.

Another troubling example that attorneys see in automobile accidents is when, immediately after an accident, someone says he is "okay" without realizing he has suffered an injury. After an accident, it usually takes a few moments for you to regain your wits and check yourself to see how you feel. If you seem to be okay and someone asks if you need assistance, you may respond: "No, I am okay." or "No, I am not injured; I am fine." After the rush of adrenaline wears off and you try to get out of bed the next morning, however, you realize that you can barely move! Oftentimes, the pain becomes worse days after the accident. You may have suffered a subtle neck or back injury that does not manifest symptoms for a day or two. While you may have felt okay initially after the accident, you actually suffered a trauma to your muscles, tendons, discs, or even bones. Just as with statements implying your acceptance of responsibility for an accident, you must also be cautious with post-accident statements to the effect that you are not injured or you are feeling fine. Instead, it is better to say that you think you are okay (if that is the case), but it is best that you go to the hospital to be examined by a doctor after any serious accident. This not only ensures that you will get immediate medical attention, but will also help document your condition should it worsen over time.

In those cases where a person initially believes that he is fine and then discovers that this is not the case, he should generally notify the other side's insurance company as soon as possible that he sustained an injury. If you are represented by an attorney, this notice should be given through your attorney.

Of course, if you clearly are injured in the accident, it is important that you seek treatment with a doctor immediately. If you wait days or even weeks to see a doctor for the first time, an insurance adjuster will contend that your pain did not result from the accident, but some other cause. It is not sufficient for you to make personal notes of your symptoms. There must be medical documentation to substantiate your claims. Your personal injury claim will be much stronger if you seek medical attention the moment your health condition changes and the doctor documents in his records each complaint and symptom that you are experiencing as a result of the accident.

WHAT IF THE AT-FAULT DRIVER DOESN'T HAVE ENOUGH INSURANCE COVERAGE FOR MY INJURIES?

Another landmine I see in personal injury cases is related to the amount of available automobile insurance coverage. Most states have statutory requirements for automobile insurance stating the minimum amount of liability insurance that a driver is required to carry. In North Carolina, drivers are required to have only $30,000 of liability insurance. Following an accident, a three-day hospital stay may cost as much as $30,000. If the driver who caused the accident carried only the minimum amount of insurance, you may be limited to a recovery of $30,000, especially if the at-fault driver is not a wealthy person with no assets greater than $30,000. If your injuries are substantial, $30,000 will not begin to cover your medical treatment and future costs. You can prevent this from being the end of the story by purchasing what is called "Underinsured Motorist Coverage" (UIM) from your own insurance company. You pay a modest additional premium for UIM coverage, which is a great way to prevent being caught short when the other driver doesn't have enough coverage to pay for your injuries and other losses.

Many people make the mistake of shopping for the cheapest automobile insurance coverage without realizing that they have an easy, cheap, way to protect themselves from drivers who only have the minimum automobile insurance coverage. In North Carolina, hundreds of thousands of dollars in UIM coverage can be purchased for less than $20 per month. However, most people ask for the cheapest policy and fail to protect themselves and their families from involvement in an automobile accident with a driver lacking sufficient insurance to cover their injuries or losses. UIM protects you if you are hurt!

For example, if your damages exceed $30,000, and the at-fault driver has the minimum coverage ($30,000), then your own insurance coverage will "kick in" to pay for expenses such as medical bills, lost wages, pain and suffering, permanent disability, and even funeral costs in the event of a death. Typically, UIM coverage is very inexpensive in relation to the amount of coverage provided.

DOCUMENT, DOCUMENT, DOCUMENT – WHETHER OR NOT YOU HAVE A LAWYER REPRESENTING YOU

Most people also do not realize that, if you fail to properly document your injuries, the amount of insurance will not matter because you may not be able to establish a successful claim without adequate documentation. It is important to write down everything and to take pictures. As time passes, it is difficult to recall all of the details surrounding an accident. We might think that an accident was such a horrible thing that we could never forget even the smallest detail, but as time passes, we do. Memories fade! For people who are going to be in a long recovery phase and endure many treatments, it is critically important to document everything that happens from the time of the accident through to the settlement or the trial of the case. Let me give you some examples.

After you are involved in an automobile accident, write down everything you can remember as soon as possible: how the accident happened, what the other driver did or said, weather conditions, passengers in any of the vehicles, any other vehicles present, etc. In a medical malpractice case, other specific details matter: what did the doctor say when he revealed information to you, were others present in the room (i.e., a nurse or your spouse), what were the doctor's instructions or recommenddations, etc. Documenting the facts is very important when trying to prove that someone else is at fault for your injuries. You will also want to document your every exchange with the opposing party, his attorney, and his insurance company. For example, if you begin receiving calls from an insurance adjuster, keep a detailed journal to document each call by date, the caller's name, the reason for the call, the phone number, and what was discussed.

If you should receive an arrangement of flowers from the other driver with a note or card, keep that card as evidence. If the other driver sends you an email or a message on Facebook, write it down in your journal and print the page for evidence. Most importantly, document your injuries and keep clear records of the losses incurred by you due to the accident. Keep all medical bills together, keep a list of every medical provider, keep documentation of lost wages, print evidence that you had to use vacation time for missed time at work, and keep the explanation of benefits forms (EOBs) received from your health insurance company.

Using photographs as documentation is also very important. If you are in an automobile accident, take pictures of all the vehicles involved—up close, at a distance, and from different angles. If the steering wheel was cracked or the airbag deployed as a result of the accident, take pictures of it. Go back to the scene of the accident and take pictures of any skid marks, the roadway itself, road signs, and anything else you think may be relevant. You should document everything you can with photographs and videos. If you were physically injured, take photographs of the injuries--bruises, cuts, stitches, and casts—as well as the healing process. This is very important for bruises since those will heal without leaving behind any evidence.

Documenting how an injury is healing, or not healing, can help prove your personal injury claim. Make sure to print the photographs and have several backup digital copies in case one or more copies are destroyed or lost. If you have an attorney, the attorney will likely handle these items for you and will help you understand what should be documented in your case.

Another helpful tactic in personal injury cases is to make a video explaining what your life was like before the accident and how it is different after. For example, if both of your arms are in casts, have someone make a video showing that you cannot write, feed yourself, or get dressed without assistance. Showing a video to a jury is much more compelling than simply telling the jury members you could not, for example, feed yourself. Showing someone feeding you as if you were an infant speaks volumes to the severity of your injuries and the disruption they caused to your life. Juries like to "see" what happened much more than just hearing about what happened. I cannot stress enough how important it is to document every-thing in writing, photos, and videos!

BUT NOT ON FACEBOOK!

The subject of photographs naturally leads me to the next topic: social media and its role in personal injury cases. We live in a world where individuals document their lives by posting photographs and "statuses" to social media sites like Facebook, Instagram, and Twitter. Those photographs and any statements you post can be used against you in a personal injury case. We recommend to our clients that they avoid using social media while they are trying to resolve their personal injury claim. Some people think we are being too extreme, but I disagree. It is not at all unusual in large personal injury cases for an insurance company to hire a private investigator to follow the claimant, just to "catch" him playing golf or tennis, driving a car, or going out with friends. Since that method of detection is expensive, many insurance companies are now turning to social media to do the work for them. Finding the claimant's Facebook page or information on other social media sites and then using the pictures posted by either the claimant or a friend as evidence, is becoming quite common.

While you may think that unfair, the opposing side is entitled to your social media information if you file a lawsuit to recover damages from an accident. The sad part is that you may not be doing anything wrong. But sometimes pictures can be used to create a false impression and by then the damage is already done. Therefore, we advise our clients to be very, very careful not to give a false impression by posts on their Facebook pages or other social media profiles and, if possible, to avoid all social networking while the case is being resolved. It can be devastating to have a completely innocent activity used to hurt you unfairly.

INJURIES FROM ASBESTOS DUST

In addition to the typical personal injury cases that my firm handles, from automobile accidents to worker's compensation injuries, we also have a long history of handling asbestos litigation. For those who are not familiar with asbestos, it is a mineral fiber that was used prior to the 1970s, mainly as thermal insulation and in construction, and is now used on a limited basis for other purposes. Asbestos has caused very serious medical conditions such as mesothelioma, which is an incurable cancer that often takes the life of the patient within a short time after diagnosis. The only known cause of mesothelioma is asbestos exposure.

Other types of cancer linked to asbestos exposure include: lung cancer, colon cancer, and esophageal cancer. It also causes asbestosis, a non-malignant but very serious and progressive incurable condition of the lungs. When people think of personal injury claims, they may not think about diseases resulting from chemical or dust exposure being litigated as personal injury cases. However, I believe that people should be made more aware of these types of personal injuries.

It is not uncommon for our firm to represent clients who, when first diagnosed with mesothelioma, reported to their doctors they had never been exposed to asbestos. However, upon careful questioning, multiple sources of potential exposure to asbestos are uncovered. One example that comes to mind is a 70-year-old person who developed lung cancer without an obvious exposure to asbestos. After asking certain questions, the asbestos exposure becomes evident: "Did you ever work on the brakes or clutch of your car?" "Did you ever remodel a kitchen by removing the vinyl flooring?" "Did you ever put up sheet rock with a wet joint compound and sand the joints after it dried?" "Did you work in a facility where there was steam or other hot processes?" Often people are exposed to asbestos without ever realizing it! Unfortunately, it does not require much asbestos exposure to develop mesothelioma. Anyone diagnosed with mesothelioma should consult a qualified, experienced mesothelioma attorney who will investigate the patient's background to determine all of the potential asbestos exposure that he may have had.

Many other chemicals to which individuals are exposed, occupationally or otherwise, may cause disease. For example, benzene is a common ingredient in many solvents that can cause leukemia. Therefore, if you or someone you know is diagnosed with leukemia, it could be the result of benzene exposure. You should seek the advice of an attorney who handles personal injury cases of this type because you may be eligible for payment of medical bills and lost wages, as well as compensation for pain and suffering.

The reason we hear so much about asbestos diseases is because a large number of manufacturers chose to continue using asbestos in their products, even though they knew it was dangerous to humans. It is tragic when companies make decisions that harm workers or the public to boost their own profits. These cases often produce large verdicts when taken to trial because jurors get very angry when they hear about a company knowingly putting its employees or the public at risk for profit. It is truly a national tragedy, because most of the diseases that develop from asbestos exposure take 20 to 40 years to manifest. By that time, most of these individuals are receiving Medicare. As a result of misguided corporate decisions, our Medicare system is required to absorb the cost of treating asbestos patients who need medical care such as chemotherapy, radiation, breathing treatments, oxygen supplies, CT scans, and expensive surgeries. Unfortunately, asbestos product manufacturers and suppliers have, through their indifference to the well-being of others, unfairly shifted the burden of paying these costs to our government and the taxpayers.

DRUG AND MEDICAL DEVICE CASES

Other personal injury cases handled by my firm involve medical devices and pharmaceuticals. These cases usually involve drugs that have been placed on the market without adequate testing, or medical devices that have been inserted into an individual's body and turn out to cause problems or require recall. The producing companies often know that the products or drugs cause problems, but fail to warn the public or the Food and Drug Administration (FDA) in a timely manner.

A current example is the ongoing litigation surrounding metal-on-metal hip implants. This was a new technology that was developed after the year 2000. Problems can occur when the metal hip joint and the metal ball rub against each other. Metal is then released into the person's body which passes through the bloodstream and into the lymph system. It can severely damage the tissue in the area of the hip implant. Patients experience metal poisoning as a result of having the metal-on-metal hip implant and often have to endure additional pain and surgery to remove the defective hip.

Other recent examples include faulty pacemakers and defective pharmaceutical drugs. If a pacemaker fails to activate when needed, it can sometimes cause catastrophic results. With regard to pharmaceuticals, the herbal drug L-Tryptophan caused many people, who purchased it as a sleep aid, to suffer muscle damage. If a manufacturer did not properly and adequately inform the public and the government with respect to a defective drug (either prescription or over-the-counter) or medical device, victims may be able to receive compensation for injuries resulting from using the drug or the medical device. Your attorney will be trying to recover compensation for your medical bills, lost wages, pain and suffering, and disability. In instances of death, the attorney would seek to recover damages for loss of life, lifetime wage loss of the deceased, medical expenses, funeral expenses, pain and suffering of the deceased, in addition to the value of the deceased's relationships with his or her loved ones.

WHAT IF I WAS INJURED BY A DOCTOR OR HOSPITAL?

Switching gears, let me talk about medical malpractice cases. Each state is a little different in applying its laws with regard to errors made by physicians, hospitals, nurses, and nursing homes. In North Carolina, as in most states, a claimant must be able to prove that the doctor or individual who was responsible for the error violated the "standard of care." That does not mean that a doctor just had something happen that resulted in a bad outcome. It also does not mean that someone may have made a small, inconsequential mistake. It means, rather, that there was a significant deviation from what the doctor should have done in that situation; what most doctors would have done in the same or a similar situation. Consequently, medical malpractice cases are more difficult to prove than most other negligence cases, such as your average automobile accident case.

For example, suppose a patient develops an infection following a procedure and contacts our office regarding whether he has a medical malpractice claim. Generally speaking, if something is a known consequence or a known risk of a particular medical procedure, the patient will not be able to recover damages for medical malpractice in North Carolina. On the other hand, in this example, if the infection was not properly evaluated and treated, causing harm to the patient, this would be considered a breach of the standard of care and could be pursued.

Unfortunately, what seems very serious to one person may be viewed as relatively minor by other people. If a patient had minor scarring as a result of a medical error, it might be difficult to find a medical malpractice attorney to take your case. Even though that seems unfair, what the public needs to understand is that, in order to win a medical malpractice case, you first must be able to prove that the doctor breached the standard of care. In order to do that, you must have experts, who are medical doctors themselves, who are willing to testify under oath that the doctor did something in error that violated the standard of care established for doctors who are performing that particular procedure in your community. You must first get past this difficult hurdle before you can even begin to try to prove to what extent you were damaged because you had minor scarring (i.e. wages lost from a modeling career).

In medical malpractice cases, claimants must understand that a cost-benefit analysis must be conducted by the attorney to determine if the case is worth taking to trial. Medical malpractice cases are very expensive to take to court and prove. Most attorneys will not accept a medical malpractice case unless it's a clear case of malpractice and the damages are very significant.

One reason these cases are so costly is that they require the testimony of expert witnesses (other doctors). The doctor facing the alleged medical malpractice claim can usually find local doctors who are willing to testify that he did nothing wrong and that he met the standard of care. In most cases, however, the claimant must hire expert witnesses from another city or even another state, because local doctors do not want to testify against doctors in their own area. A claimant may be faced with hiring experts costing $10,000 to try to prove that malpractice occurred, when the claimant has only $5,000 in medical bills. In this instance, it would not be prudent to proceed with a medical malpractice case, because the cost of proving the case would far exceed the amount of damages sustained. It is not that the error did not occur or did not rise to the level of malpractice, it is simply that the costs involved in trying the medical malpractice case make it impractical.

Jurors are another factor that must be taken into account in medical malpractice cases. Jurors generally do not like to believe that doctors make mistakes. Some jurors believe that, because doctors are working to help people, they sometimes deserve a break when things go wrong. In general, jurors do not side with the person who was injured. In over 80% of the medical malpractice cases that are tried, North Carolina jurors will side with the doctor or medical provider.

A person injured as a result of medical malpractice may believe he has a great case and he does not understand why lawyer after lawyer has turned down his case, why no one is willing to represent him in a medical malpractice claim. He must understand that there are several practical aspects, in addition to whether malpractice has actually taken place, that must be considered when an attorney reviews a potential medical malpractice case. It is not that the attorney is necessarily saying that the person does not have a good case, but perhaps that the damages in the case simply do not justify the investment of time and costs.

Medical malpractice cases can be those that arise from an error (such as an overdose or surgical mistake) while others may be based on what is referred to as a "failure to diagnose" or "failure to treat." An individual's specific circumstances must be reviewed to make sure that the medical personnel (doctors, nurses, hospital providers) have evaluated the appropriate treatment options. Medical malpractice cases may occur because someone did something wrong, but they may also occur because someone failed to do something they should have done, resulting in a serious adverse result. For example, assume that Jane also goes to the doctor for her annual mammogram. There is a suspicious spot on the mammogram, but no one follows up with Jane to get it evaluated further. She comes back the next year and her undiagnosed breast cancer has now spread throughout her body. In this scenario, a medical malpractice case could be termed a "failure to diagnose" claim. However, such types of cases can also be very difficult to prove. Jane's attorney would need to find expert witnesses who would testify that earlier treatment would have made a difference in the outcome of Jane's disease. The expert would need to be able to articulate and prove to the satisfaction of the court that the outcome would have changed for the better if the diagnosis had been made sooner rather than later. Being able to prove that an earlier diagnosis would have made a difference in the outcome is an essential element in proving a failure to diagnose case.

HOW CAN I GET ADVICE FROM A LAWYER FOR FREE? OR WHAT IF I CAN'T AFFORD A LAWYER?

Most people we represent have never before needed a lawyer and do not know which lawyer to call when they sustain an injury and need advice. I believe that claimants should be able to get some information from lawyers without charge. My firm, and most good personal injury firms in North Carolina provide free consultations for personal injury clients. If you are involved in an automobile accident and call our office, we will tell you the next steps to take without charging you a fee. Therefore, people should make those calls and not be afraid to seek the counsel of an attorney to find out what steps they need to take after suffering an injury.

If a claimant does decide to retain our firm, we will take the case on a contingency fee basis. We never ask a personal injury client to write us a check or charge them a retainer fee. Our firm does all of the work on the case and advances the case expenses, never charging the client unless and until money is recovered from the other party. To me, this is an excellent way for any person, regardless of his or her means, to have experienced representation in his or her personal injury claim. Rather than basing our fee on the client's ability to pay, we base it on our ability to be a successful in resolving the client's case.

Attorneys are trying to level the playing field between the parties. Insurance companies are typically multi-million dollar corporations that employ hundreds of attorneys and thousands of adjusters, doing everything in their power to minimize how much the insurance company must pay the injured party to settle the claim. Having a great law firm on your side as your voice is essential to gaining the justice you deserve.

(This content should be used for informational purposes only. It does not create an attorney-client relationship with any reader and should not be construed as legal advice. If you need legal advice, please contact an attorney in your community who can assess the specifics of your situation.)

4

IF YOU WANT MORE MONEY, HIRE A PERSONAL INJURY ATTORNEY

by Gerald R. Stahl, Esq.

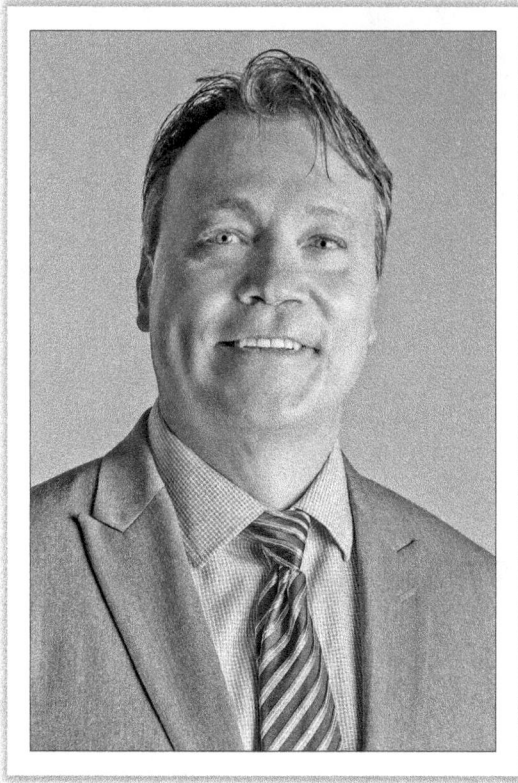

Gerald R. Stahl, Esq.
Law Offices of Gerald R. Stahl
Grand Rapids, Michigan

Gerald R. Stahl is a Grand Rapids, Michigan based Trial Lawyer that has been successfully representing victims of auto and truck accidents for over 32 years. He is committed to helping client's put their lives back together after a serious accident. He is relentless in his pursuit of achieving maximum financial recovery for his clients. He is a dedicated member of The American Association for Justice and a Fellow in The National College of Advocacy. He is rated 10 out 10, "Superb" by Avvo. He is recognized as a top 100 litigation attorney in

Michigan for 2014 by The American Society of Legal Advocates. He was awarded Top 100 Lawyers by the National Trial Lawyers for 2014.

IF YOU WANT MORE MONEY, HIRE A PERSONAL INJURY ATTORNEY

The average person does not have the experience or time to handle most elements of a personal injury claim. The attorney's job is to perform difficult duties and apprise the client of progress to eliminate needless stress resulting from claims and facilitate a speedy recovery. I have been practicing for 32 years and there is solid evidence that clients are awarded more money with an attorney's help than without—even after paying attorney's fees. Although economic reward is, perhaps, the most important reason to hire an attorney, there are many other important reasons to hire a personal injury attorney as well.

Automobile accidents seriously traumatize those involved, physically altering their lives while causing often paralyzing and emotional distress. Fear and anxiety ravage accident victims and families. They worry about mental and physical recovery, medical bills, and lost wages. They want their lives to return to normal but feel helpless amidst the strange medical machines that beep; a constant reminder of sometimes irreparable damage.

Accident victims deserve compensation for their damages. Without the assistance of a competent attorney, however, recompense for physical and emotional suffering will likely be minimal. Most accident victims do not have the experience and time necessary to deal with insurance companies, insurance adjusters, and the red tape involved when dealing with a personal injury claim. The assistance of a caring attorney with years of education and expertise will relieve accident victims and their worried families of unnecessary burdens and greatly increase the likelihood of financial recompense.

We deal with these situations every day and we have the legal expertise to handle personal injury claims. Most people claim to understand no-fault insurance and premises liability, but they cannot clearly and comprehensively explain such concepts. Limited knowledge and an inability to clearly and convincingly present a case in court can seriously hurt many accident victims who proceed without an attorney. Knowing the law is extremely important when dealing with a personal injury case. Accident victims must demonstrate to an insurance company that they know the law and are prepared to take their claim to court, if necessary, to obtain a fair and just settlement for themselves and their families. Since most accident victims cannot do that, hiring an attorney should be their first priority.

Accident victims need an attorney on their side from the beginning. The attorney will identify the responsible parties and notify the owners and insurance companies of a claim. Attorneys request copies of police reports, hire investigators, investigate the scene, and take photographs of the injuries and the vehicles. In some cases, an attorney might utilize the services of an accident reconstruction expert. Your attorney will deal with the numerous and often tedious claim forms that must be completed and filed with various companies and agencies. Personal injury attorneys must obtain copies of the medical records and analyze those records, which can be a difficult process. I have had clients tell me that they did not realize the extent of their injury until after I completed the review of their medical records. The medical records are correlated and highlighted to call attention to the important and relevant sections that will be used as part of the negotiation process. Of course, the attorney is negotiating with the insurance company, drafting settlement proposals and preparing for trial if necessary. Without timely intervention from a competent and caring attorney, physical damages may remain forever, and monetary damages may never surface.

SUBROGATION RIGHTS – DON'T SETTLE YOUR CLAIM WITHOUT KNOWING WHAT THEY ARE

The claims process is extremely complex and tedious. Subrogation rights are a primary and necessary example. When people are involved in an accident where a third-party insurance company may be liable for damages, their health insurance provider will often put accident sufferers and their attorney on notice of their subrogation claim. In other words, the insurance company that pays victims' medical bills expects to be reimbursed from the settlement proceeds they receive from a third-party insurance company. When accident victims receive this letter, the first step is to determine if the company is entitled to a subrogation claim. Often, at least in Michigan, they are not.

For example, in an automobile accident, the insurance company that paid the medical bills would not be entitled to a subrogation claim because we allow for third-party bodily injury settlements (or pain and suffering) claims only. Companies are not entitled to reimbursement from this type of settlement. Conversely, premises liability claims such as slipping on a banana peel or head trauma from a falling brick are subject to subrogation claims. The complexity of these claims makes procuring a competent and caring attorney essential for most people.

A knowledgeable attorney will decide the merits of a subrogation claim and make strong efforts to negotiate a lesser amount to settle the claim.

For example, the person responsible for the accident has insurance coverage with a $250,000 policy limit. However, the medical bills paid by the victim's insurance company exceed $300,000. The victim's own insurance company seeks subrogation claim is for excess of $300,000 out of the settlement. In this instance, if the victim accepted settlement without negotiating the subrogation claim then he would recover nothing. That is hardly justice!

Thankfully, many people hire an attorney. The attorney would contact the insurance company for the victim and explain that because the subrogation claim exceeds the settlement offer, the case must now go to trial where there is always a risk of losing. The attorney would go on to explain to the company that if it were willing to accept 10 cents on the dollar, they could settle the case and the company would assuredly receive $30,000. If the case were to go to trial, they may receive nothing. A good attorney would also add that the client will suffer for the rest of their life with this injury and deserves the $220,000 settlement as a matter of justice. Of course, a sage attorney would not consider negotiating an easily-winnable case.

There is always the possibility of losing. However, my policy is take only cases I believe in; cases where people have been wronged by the negligence of a third party and sustained serious or significant personal injuries. This helps us achieve the best results for the client.

Filing a personal injury claim is a complicated and laborious process. For instance, if a complainant files a premises liability claim after being injured on another's property, the owner of the property may not accept fault. The owner may allege that the injury was the complainant's fault because the complainant's claim, if justified, will greatly raise the owner's insurance rates. Imagine, for example, that you fall on an ice patch on another's property. Fearful of the consequences, the property owner explains in detail why you must bear all responsibility. The owner goes to great lengths to deny responsibility. The owner's anger and vehement denial of responsibility immediately pits you against him and his insurance company. You are all alone against two adversaries who do not want to help you recover the dignity you deserve. That is one reason you need an attorney. You need to even the odds.

Next, a complainant may have a case where the liability is clearly on the defendant's shoulders but the insurance company is worried about the amount of damages it may have to pay. For example, a client suffers multiple injuries (i.e., fractured ankle, broken ribs, rotator cuff injury, etc.) in a trucking accident. The insurance company immediately begins to look at what their potential exposure is because they have a 5 million dollar insurance policy sitting out there. The adversarial relationship in this case would be determining the value of the claim.

The insurance company makes money by paying as little as possible on claims. The insurance company profits, though, at the expense of the accident victim. For example, imagine a driver is hit by a truck that runs a red light. The victim suffers from serious injuries that greatly impact ability to work and future earnings. Unable to pay exorbitant medical bills, the victim wastes away in poverty and isolation, unable to do once enjoyable activities such as hiking and shooting hoops. As the accident and forced physical inactivity continue to ravage this once healthy, productive life, the insurance company continues to prosper as the victim lives in misery.

After 32 years of practice, I have seen many cases where people are in wheelchairs or using walkers 10 to 15 years after an accident because their injuries caused other health issues later in life. A competent and caring attorney can increase the likelihood that an accident victim will prosper despite the profit-seeking penchant of their adversary, the insurance company. There is no way to escape the adversarial clash with insurance companies, but we will fight tirelessly to get you the compensation you deserve.

LEGAL LANDMINES: HELPING CLIENTS LOOK BEFORE THEY LEAP

Dealing with an insurance company is like trying to navigate through a minefield. Insurance companies use tactics to divert victims or trick them during the claims process. For example, many insurance companies maliciously use information found in police reports. Often, a police report will contain false information or erroneous conclusions. I just settled a case where the plaintiff was injured in an at-fault accident. The driver of a semi-truck crashed through a red light. In that particular case, my client wanted to go to a hospital on the other side of town; however, the ambulance driver wanted to transport him to the nearest hospital. The police officer got out of his car and spoke with the ambulance driver. After a minute, the officer asked my client if he was okay and my client responded, "Yes, I'm alright." The police officer and ambulance left. My client developed shortness of breath and pain throughout his side. He had suffered nine broken ribs and a collapsed lung. Even though the ambulance came back to transport him to the hospital, the police report read "no injuries" and "no ambulance."

Another example of problems with police reports that I witnessed occurred in a tragic motorcycle accident case that I handled successfully. A young man, who had a history of speeding, was riding his motorcycle in rural Michigan. On this particular day, his girlfriend was riding on the back of the motorcycle, so he was traveling at a slower speed than normal. A tractor pulling a manure spreader pulled out in front of him. The young man was killed and his girlfriend suffered major injuries, including serious head trauma. The officer at the scene concluded that my client's excessive speed caused the accident. We had to retain the services of an accident reconstruction expert to prove that the officer's conclusion was incorrect. The officer had calculated speed erroneously, using faulty methods. Moreover, the officer should have known it is illegal to enter the roadway in front of a motorcycle once one sees it. The insurance company finally admitted fault on the farmer's part and settled. These are just two of the many examples that prove how a police report can be a landmine in a victim's case.

Another landmine that we encounter is with medical records and emergency room reports. One of my clients was injured while walking in front of her apartment complex on an ill-maintained sidewalk. When I reviewed the emergency room report, it stated that she was injured when she tripped over a doghouse. However, we had pictures of the sidewalk and testimony from witnesses who helped the fallen victim after the unfortunate accident. Moreover, the apartment complex prohibits dog ownership! Despite overwhelming evidence of the sidewalk fiasco, we had to immediately deal with that erroneous statement before moving on with the case. Without an attorney to review the records and fight for justice, this landmine could have exploded, leaving this poor woman—this innocent victim of a wayward walkway—penniless.

Medical records are rife with inaccuracies and for a myriad of reasons. Doctors can misdiagnose a patient or fail to provide a diagnosis at all. Some doctors will note in the records that they have released the patient to return to work, but forget to revise their notation when they change their mind. It is nearly impossible to get a doctor or police officer to change a report and impossible to get the hospital to change its records. Attorneys must prove that the records are wrong. Without an attorney's help, accident victims may lose the case, and that is an unfortunate record that cannot be changed either.

The personalities of insurance adjusters and insurance companies are also landmines that we encounter in personal injury work. Insurance companies have personalities, some better than others. For example, some insurance companies are willing to work with attorneys and their clients to resolve claims while other insurance companies will fight every claim from the beginning. When the insurance company fights, preparation helps an attorney win good settlements for clients.

There are some decent insurance companies out there and I have achieved excellent results from those companies. But what is required is to develop a reputation with those insurance companies as an attorney who is serious and prepared. They know they cannot use insurance buzzwords and idioms such as, "We need to round-table this" or, "I don't have authority for this" to avoid the claim. It is difficult for many people to discern if insurance companies are being honest or if they are stalling.

However, I have been around long enough to know which insurance companies are going to settle a case and for approximately what amount. My experience helps to disengage this otherwise dangerous landmine.

Speaking of dangerous landmines, clients rarely understand the valuation of a case. The goal of a personal injury attorney is to put clients back in their before-accident position. I will use an example to clarify the concept. A man had his leg and ankle broken. He had plates, screws, and internal fixtures throughout his leg and ankle. He had to have multiple surgeries to try to repair the damage. He is a roofer and will probably never be able to work again. It is impossible for an attorney or any mortal being to restore his physical health. However, we try to get him monetary compensation for his injuries. To one insurance company, that injury could be worth $250,000. However, another insurance company may value the claim at $500,000 or $750,000. There is a broad range of settlement values. It is difficult, therefore, for accident victims to determine the "value" of their injuries. Unlike vehicular damage, the body has no "Kelly Blue Book" to determine monetary value.

The reason there is such a wide range in values is that everybody is different. Everybody has different jobs, feelings, and emotions. The attorney must take the time to get to know the client, and the client's expectations, to ensure sensitivity to the client's problems. The attorney must also know the insurance companies and know when to fight and when not to fight. Sometimes, the insurance company will lowball attorneys. I have seen a case where insurance companies have offered $60,000 to settle a case and we beat them out of $990,000! Clients need to understand that it is a difficult process and that it is impossible to fully restore the pre-accident health and happiness they once enjoyed. Insurance companies will often try to add insult to injury with lowball offers. Attorneys must work tirelessly to ensure clients receive the settlements they deserve.

Another problem some people run into is state minimum insurance coverage. Some states allow perilously low insurance coverage. Therefore, in theory, a person could be hit by a college student who is texting while driving and carrying the state's minimum insurance coverage. After suffering a broken arm and permanent facial scarring, the victim attempts to sue for damages. However, in an even greater reversal of fortune, the victim discovers the defendant's insurance payout is $20,000 maximum! In this unfortunate case, the victim's damages greatly exceed the defendant's insurance limits. Even with an attorney, the only recourse a victim may have is uninsured/underinsured motorist coverage. Without it, the victim may be victimized yet again.

If you have $100,000 in Uninsured or Underinsured Motorist coverage, you will receive the first $20,000 from the other driver's insurance company but then you can collect up to an additional $80,000 from your own insurance company. Let's assume that you also carry the state minimum requirements; you are now left with only the $20,000 from the other driver because there will not be any equity or assets for you to recover in a lawsuit. So this is something that you should be aware of and plan for when deciding the coverage amounts for your own insurance policy. With premises liability claims, most insurance policies have $1,000,000 in coverage. For a dog bite case, the homeowner probably has up to $300,000 in bodily injury coverage. Most people understand that they need to have higher automobile coverage, but because of difficult economic times, they do not have the coverage they truly need.

Another landmine I see involves statements given to insurance companies. This is another excellent reason to hire a personal injury attorney immediately following an accident. Insurance companies like to get their foot in the door after an injury so that they can talk to the injured person before they have a chance to hire an attorney. They want to use any incriminating statements that the person may make to diminish or devalue the claim. I had an exceptionally serious case where my client actually told the insurance company that he would be meeting with me in the hospital. While I was there, the insurance adjuster audaciously showed up. She turned around and left when she realized I was there. However, she had the nerve to come to the victim's hospital room before I could speak with him.

What the insurance company wants to do is get a statement from the victim, which they can use against them later in the case. For instance, let us assume that the insurance adjuster asks you several questions, such as, "Were you texting while driving?", "Was the radio on?", and "Was the light yellow?" You are still recovering from your injuries and trying your best to remember, so you say that you do not remember about the light. You were not texting, the radio was on, but you just do not remember the light. So the insurance adjuster says, "Well, the light was yellow," and you say, "Well, it could have been. I don't remember. It could have been." Even though we have three witnesses who say the light was green, your statement is still out there that it could have been yellow. The insurance adjuster records your claim. A permanent notation, this erroneous statement, given in an injury-induced fog, can hinder your chances of receiving a fair settlement. Your unwitting statement may halt the wheels of justice.

Insurance companies also look for pre-existing conditions to avoid their payment obligations. For example, a serious accident may affect the victim's spatial orientation and cause headaches and the need for eyeglasses. The insurance company may ask the victims questions, however, so they can attribute the problems to a preexisting condition: "Well, you were experiencing some of these symptoms before the accident, right? You were taking anti-depressant drugs before the accident, right?"

Even though the victim had headaches before the accident, the closed head injury causes chronic headaches that are much different from the ones before the accident. The insurance company will still try to prove the headaches are a pre-existing condition, however, all in an effort to avoid a big payout. The support of doctors who concur that the accident has caused the symptoms can greatly assist the victim's claim. Medical tests are objective evidence that can help prove a claim. If doctors are not ordering the requisite tests, the attorney can assist clients and encourage them to demand the necessary treatment.

CATASTROPHIC INJURIES FROM SEMI-TRUCK ACCIDENTS

We handle many semi-truck accident cases in my practice. Accidents involving semi-trucks result in devastating injuries. However, it is difficult to make a claim against a truck driver, his company, and the insurance carrier. There are numerous regulations and red tape that one must deal with in these types of cases. Trucks are regulated by the Federal Motor Carriers Safety Regulations, so drivers must keep daily trip logs, perform safety inspections, ensure they are not sleep deprived, and limit the number of hours they drive pursuant to the regulations.

Many different things can happen with trucks. Loads may shift while the truck is climbing a steep incline or going around sharp curves. Excessive weight may cause defective brakes. Moreover, poor and inexperienced drivers operate some trucks. I recall one case in particular. A semi-driver was on a major roadway traveling 55 mph when he ran a red light and crashed into another vehicle. My client was a passenger in the vehicle. The driver of the vehicle perished and my client suffered severe internal injuries. The driver of the semi-truck was Hispanic. When we went to the court hearing for the criminal charges against him, he had a language interpreter present. I looked at the regulations for truck drivers and one of the regulations specifically states that one must be able to speak English to drive a semi-truck. This driver could not speak English.

There are seemingly endless regulations in the Federal Motor Carrier Act (FMCA). Most people do not understand that they must read and analyze these regulations at the time of a semi-truck accident. Driver infractions may range from the obvious, such as driving while tired or intoxicated, to the more obscure, such as driving without an ability to speak English. Knowledge of the FMCA in its entirety is necessary for clients to receive a successful settlement.

There are many things that can go wrong with a semi-truck; problems undetected by the most cautious mechanics and beyond the knowledge of any truck driver. Even the failure to have proper lighting can be an issue in a truck accident case. Like the law, however, ignorance of a problem is no excuse. It does not absolve people of responsibility. One out of nine traffic fatalities involve a truck. It is devastating when these types of accidents happen. The injuries are severe, even when trucks are traveling at slower speeds. Trucking accident cases are so specialized that they require an attorney who has experience successfully litigating such cases. Such experience will help a client prosper. An attorney must know what evidence to preserve, how to write the letter that must be sent to preserve that evidence, and the regulations that govern the trucking industry. It takes much experience to aggressively pursue a wrongful death case or accident that obviously alters someone's life.

TWO MEMORABLE CASES

One case that stands out was from 1995. I handled the case with another lawyer. We shared duties equally all the way through the trial. Our client was stopped, waiting patiently to make a left hand turn once traffic had cleared. She was rear-ended by a large van, approximately the size of a UPS van. The driver of the van had looked away from traffic to look at a construction site when he struck our client's vehicle. After a co-worker took her to the hospital, our client was diagnosed with a mild head injury. During the next few months, she was treated by several different physicians for chronic back and neck pains, chronic daily headaches, and chronic photosensitivity. Even though she was a great employee and highly skilled in her position, she eventually lost her job because of the injuries she sustained in the accident. Our client spent approximately 18 months suffering from the effects of her closed head injury. The insurance company was not willing to negotiate with us so we eventually filed the lawsuit.

After filing suit, the attorneys for the insurance company, for unknown reasons, did not believe that our client sustained the injuries she claimed. Therefore, we began to take depositions from the many doctors she had seen during her lengthy medical treatment. Taking the deposition of a physician is a costly endeavor, typically costing between $500 and $5,000, depending upon the physician and the length of the deposition. However, it was necessary in this case to prove the extent of our client's injuries. Every doctor that we deposed, from the first through to the last, said the same thing: this woman has suffered terribly, but she is trying extremely hard to recover. She had so many problems and so much pain from the chronic headaches that she was unable to function as she did before the accident. Each doctor verified that our client had done everything that she was asked to do, yet she still suffered. She underwent a battery of psychological tests and neuropsychological tests and did all of the work required of her by the physicians. The results verified that she suffered a terrible injury. Privy to this information, the attorney for the insurance company had yet to offer any type of settlement.

The attorney for the insurance company had retained the services of only one expert witness. His sole expert witness did nothing but write about malingering, which is a buzzword for insurance companies. It means that the person should have gotten better but made no discernible effort to do so. The person is using the "illness" as an excuse for financial benefit. By this time, our client had returned to working part-time, making a fraction of the money she was making prior to the accident. She had to sit in a special chair, just to be able to work part-time. However, the attorney for the insurance company refused to see this individual tree of truth through his forest of faulty ideas. This woman was working at the top of her field. The accident put her at the bottom, and his sole argument was, "She is back at work!"

I will never forget the comment that the defense's sole expert witness made after the attorney I was working with finished his cross-examination; "Good questions." It was interesting, because this doctor did nothing but write about malingering. He never examined our client to render any type of diagnosis. All that he did was to examine her medical records; the same records written by our doctors that said she suffered a terrible injury, was in severe pain, and doing everything she could to recover. At the end of the case, we prevailed with a $990,000 verdict for our client.

Another personal injury case involved a semi-truck and a small vehicle. My client was a passenger in the car. When the semi-truck pulled out in front of the small car, the car's tire hit the semi-truck, causing the car to bounce up and down. My client hit her head on the ceiling of the car. She was taken to the hospital and released; however, for the next six months, she lay on her back at home, barely able to talk or even remember what she had eaten. It was not until she went to see a chiropractor that she questioned the origin of all these problems with her memory, back, and neck. He referred her to a neurologist, and my client was diagnosed with an extremely- severe brain injury. A brain injury is not something one can see, so it is difficult to diagnose until symptoms begin to present themselves to the patient. Attorneys must make genuine efforts to talk with patients and understand how the accident has changed their lives. They must be cognizant of the outward signs of distress and elicit evidence through systematic questioning.

To be a great personal injury attorney, one must move beyond monetary profit. One must genuinely want to help people who are suffering because of another's negligence. Their world has been turned upside down and attorneys must be able to see that and understand that to make the insurance company understand. Sometimes, that is not an easy task. It requires an experienced attorney to do that, especially for serious and catastrophic injury cases.

In closing, if you are seriously injured in an accident that is not your fault, it is critical that you consult with a personal injury lawyer. Personal injury lawyers normally offer a free consultation. Most attorneys accept personal injury cases on a contingency fee basis so that you will not owe anything to the attorney until and unless a monetary award is recovered on your behalf. Experienced personal injury lawyers are experts in negotiating and evaluating a case. They are trained to get you the most money possible for your claim. Most important, always talk to the lawyer before you give any statements to an insurance company or insurance adjuster.

(This content should be used for informational purposes only. It does not create an attorney-client relationship with any reader and should not be construed as legal advice. If you need legal advice, please contact an attorney in your community who can assess the specifics of your situation.)

5

$20 WOULD HAVE PREVENTED THIS TRAGEDY

by Collin D. Kennedy, Esq.

Collin D. Kennedy, Esq.
Hanshaw, Kennedy, Marquis, PLLC
Dallas, Texas

Collin Kennedy is a leading personal injury in the Dallas area. His years of experience have taught him two never-to-be-broken rules. First, to get the best result for his client, and to prepare each case like it is the most important case he will ever have. After all, in most instances, it is the most important case the client will ever have. And second, to get the best result for his client, he treats each case like he is representing the best of his friends or the closest of his family members. In other words, he takes his representation of victims personally.

110

$20 WOULD HAVE PREVENTED THIS TRAGEDY

I wanted to talk a little bit about premises liability. Premises liability generally means that when people own property, such as homes or businesses, they are liable for any damages if something happens or occurs on those premises that make it inherently unsafe for someone else to come onto the property. For example, let us hypothesize that a person is building a home, and it is open to the public, during the construction phase, for people to enter the home to look around. The staircase that is being constructed does not have any rails yet and no safety measures are in place to prevent someone from getting hurt. A family enters the home with a child who climbs the stairs and then falls striking his head, causing serious injury. Under most state laws, this would be sufficient to generate a premises liability case because the owner of that property should have realized that it was an obvious danger and taken steps to prevent an injury from occurring. However, in most cases, premises liability is actually much more complicated than this example.

I have handled several different types of premises liability cases. However, there is one case that particularly pulls on my heartstrings when I think about it. It involves a specific kind of premises liability: swimming pool drowning. Several years ago, my wife and I were adding a swimming pool in our backyard. We had little kids at the time, and we had just started the excavation of the hole when I received a frantic call at work from a mother whose two-year-old had drowned over the weekend in a swimming pool. It stopped my wife and me in our tracks as we also had a two-year-old, and we were building a swimming pool in our backyard. As we started the investigation of this claim, we found that the family lived in an apartment complex that was slightly dilapidated. When ownership of the complex changed, the new owner did not retain the services of a property manager with knowledge of swimming pools. Therefore, the swimming pool fell into disrepair, the pumps stopped working and the water had darkened. This happened in the middle of summer. There were some latches that were not in proper repair on the gate surrounding the pool. The parents were in their apartment when they realized that their son was missing and began to frantically search for him. He had only been gone a few minutes when they realized this, so he could not have gone very far. They looked in the pool, but the water was dark. So they got a pole and began to poke around the bottom but found nothing. They enlisted the help of their friends and family, but no one could find the toddler anywhere in the neighborhood. Twenty minutes later, they came back to the swimming pool area and put the pole in again—up floated the boy's body. We were amazed at how preventable this tragedy could have been by just securing the fence, draining the pool or covering the pool. It was an inherently dangerous situation that made me believe that liability was a clear-cut issue. Damages were not an issue as this was the death of a two-year-old boy. How can anyone calculate the loss of a life? Nevertheless, it was substantial. Collectability seemed to be the real issue in this case. We had what appeared to be a shoddy company that had purchased this property for a low amount, so the solvency of this company was in question.

Therefore, a significant portion of our investigation was dedicated to whether the plaintiffs would have a solvent defendant if we tried the case. The other elements of our case were very strong, so I requested the public records to determine if the apartment complex had ever been issued a citation. The frustrating part of this investigation was waiting for information because municipalities can take months to respond to a request for records. The family was frustrated, as was I, so I called the city office only to find out that they had sent the records to the wrong address. At that point, I got my keys, got into my car, drove downtown to the city office, and sat in the lobby until they produced the records.

The folder had about 15 pages, so I really did not think I would find anything; however, on page nine was a citation that read in part, "This pool is in violation of various safety regulations. If you do not cover it or drain it, we will do so, and you will be subject to significant civil penalties. You have 14 days to comply." It was on the 17th day after this notice that the little boy drowned in this pool because no one did anything in response to that letter. It was at this moment that I realized this is something that rarely happens in the practice of law; it was a Perry Mason-type of moment that you hear about in law school but never believe. To say that I held a smoking gun in my hand was an understatement. I held evidence that showed the owners knew of the extremely dangerous situation on their property and chose to do nothing about it because it was too much of a bother or because the cost to remedy the situation was more than the owners were willing to spend. All that would have been necessary to remedy the situation was for the property manager or owner to drain the swimming pool or buy a few pieces of plywood to cover the pool. They chose not to do this, and their inaction changed the trajectory of this family's life forever.

I took that letter, which was now the seminal piece of evidence in our case, and crafted it into a demand that I sent to the owner of the property. Even though the facts supporting the property owner's liability were overwhelming, I still had to face the collectability issue. This is also an example of how luck can come into play even in the area of law. I received a call one day from a lawyer with a big law firm in Texas. He informed me that he represented a gigantic Fortune 500 company who had purchased this property as part of a distressed properties portfolio a few months earlier, and they wanted to settle. We both decided that the best opportunity to work out an amicable resolution for everyone involved was to go to mediation. The night before the mediation, I was nervous because I wanted to achieve a good result for this family. No one could take a case like this without in some way becoming personally invested in the outcome, seeing the toll that a tragedy such as this takes on a family. All good attorneys treat each case as if it were their very own family's case and, by doing so, they do the best job possible for the family. This is how I came to be at Home Depot the night before the mediation.

I am by no means a carpenter—I am lucky if I can drive a nail through a board without bending the nail. Nevertheless, I went to Home Depot to purchase the materials to build a cross section of a gate. Even if the swimming pool had been in disrepair, a working gate would have prevented the toddler from drowning. I arrived at the mediation early and hid the gate that I had built under the table so that the opposing counsel could not see it until I was ready.

I began the mediation by pulling out what I had built and saying, "This cost me $27 last night at Home Depot, to get a latch that I affixed to this gate that would secure it and keep it out of the reach of a two-year-old little boy. Because your client ignored that citation letter and chose not to spend the few bucks it would have taken to prevent this, my clients lost their two-year-old child." Mediation is an adversarial process in which we present our case and then the attorneys for the opposing party present their case to defend the action or inaction of the other party. However, when I completed my presentation, I looked around the conference table. The mediator, who had been mediating cases for about 20 years and had an extremely strong personality, the army of lawyers who represented the other side, and everyone on my side of the table were all misty-eyed. Naturally, the case settled.

I tell this story because it touches on so many points in the practice of personal injury. First, the way you treat a case will have a profound effect on the result you achieve. As the lawyer, you must be invested in the case and connect with your clients to get a positive result. Second, looking at the execution of this case again, and the complexities involved in a personal injury case, this would never have been a case worth taking on had the company that owned the building been insolvent. Basically, this child would have lost his life, and there would have been no recourse for his family. Horrible incidents can take place without having the legal grounds to obtain justice. That is the unfortunate point I am making: many things must fall into place to obtain justice.

This is a case that I will never forget. The segment of gate that I built still stands in the corner of my office, and it is a constant reminder that sometimes we get jaded, tired, and frustrated. The gate reminds me that, when I get the next call or when I am dealing with the next case, the case is just as important to the next family as this child's life was important to his parents. I have to be personally invested in each case that I take, and I must treat each one as if it were my own family member's case or as if one of my own friends had been hurt, if justice is going to be served to the fullest extent that that it can be served. I keep that case memento in my office—right there in front of me—so that every time I am talking to a client on the telephone, or I have one sitting in front of me in my office, that gate gives me perspective.

SOCIAL MEDIA CAN DESTROY YOUR CASE

I would like to discuss how social media has had a huge impact on personal injury cases. In fact, it is not just personal injury law that has been impacted by social media. Social media is impacting all areas of the law in one way or another. My favorite story about this subject dates back to when social media was just getting started. Before Facebook was created, one of the first popular social media websites, especially for kids, was called MySpace. I had a family come into my office with a unique personal injury claim. The daughter had been to the movies with friends. When the movie ended, she and her friends exited the theater, and they were walking in the parking lot when a teenage friend—a young man—scooped up the girl and ran across the parking lot towards the car. He tripped over a parking block, dropped her and she hit her head on the parking block. As a result, she suffered an olfactory injury, which caused the loss of her sense of smell and taste. It was an odd injury that most people do not hear much about, so we started to look into it.

It would be tragic to be born without a sense of smell or taste: never to taste fresh, buttery popcorn or smell chocolate chip cookies baking in the oven. This poor teenager had grown up with a sense of smell and taste but now was claiming that she had lost the ability to smell any thing or taste anything. There is a safety issue involved, too; because if someone without the sense of smell is sleeping, this person will not be able to smell smoke if the house is on fire. So the person is at a greater risk of harm than someone with the ability to smell.

We began to investigate the case by taking her to a neurologist so that he could educate me on this type of injury, since I had never handled this type of case. The neurologist said that there were no objective tests to measure the senses of smell and taste because doctors are basically relying on the people they are testing to be honest when they report that they cannot smell or taste what is being placed in front of them. At the time, I was not skeptical because I was getting anecdotal information from the girl and her parents that she had lost the sense of smell and taste. As the case progressed, I really learned my lesson. This incident occurred during the introduction of social media into the mainstream; opposing counsel sent a subpoena for the records of my client's MySpace page. I had not even thought to ask her about it because social media was something that had just begun to be popular, but now I ask in every case. Now, when I meet with clients, I want to know every social media website that they use: Facebook, Twitter, LinkedIn, etc.

"I am going to look at each one and you are going to provide me with all of the information to do this because I want to make sure there is nothing in there that contradicts anything you are telling me (i.e., pictures, statements, comments, etc.)."

When I received the subpoena, I called opposing counsel and asked what this was all about, and he responded, "Well, I'm not positive but you'll see."

After reviewing her MySpace page, we discovered that about three months after the accident in which she claimed to have lost her senses of smell and taste, she posted on MySpace something along the lines of, "Man, that coffee smells good this morning!" or "Well, I just enjoyed a fresh cup of coffee. It tasted wonderful." That was the end of the case. I called my client and questioned her, but she had been dishonest with me, either about the degree to which she may have lost her senses or about whether she actually had at all.

To this day, I am still amazed, but it was a wake-up call for me. I invested a lot of time and effort into that case and if I had only known then what I know now about social media, I would have handled that case differently from the very beginning. It was embarrassing, and I am the first to admit it, but it was a great learning experience for me. Now, when I meet with clients, I have it stated plainly on my forms that they must give me everything related to their social media sites. I will not accept a case unless they allow me to see their social media sites because I think it is a red flag if they do not. I do not want to be burned like that ever again. People will say anything on social media websites. Because they do say anything and they have the propensity to share things that you would not believe they would want to be public information, it often becomes relevant in cases that I take on. That was certainly a learning-the-hard-way example that I wish I'd had the foresight to investigate myself. However, we are talking about ten years ago when social media was a very new concept in our world.

THE COMPLEXITIES OF A PERSONAL INJURY CLAIM

I've touched upon a couple of memorable stories over the years which illustrate the various stages of a personal injury case, but I would like to further discuss the phases and complexities of navigating a personal injury claim. I believe there are many misconceptions regarding the workings of a personal injury case because, for the most part, a person may only be involved in one case of this nature during an entire lifetime. The first phase of a personal injury case is the investigation of the claim. In my opinion, this is the most important phase in a personal injury case, and many attorneys fail to adequately investigate a claim prior to agreeing to take the case. I prefer not to commit to taking a personal injury case until I have had the opportunity to thoroughly investigate the matter. Rarely do I commit to representing a client after an initial consultation. This method of work, I think, is a result of four years of working as a prosecutor in Houston at the beginning of my legal career. There is a lot of investigation involved in a criminal case, and the experience I gained as a prosecutor has served me well in the transition from a criminal practice to a personal injury practice.

Many elements make up the investigation of a personal injury claim. The first step I take is to request a copy of the police report, if one was filed. The police report has valuable information that can assist me in my investigation of the claim, such as the responsible party's insurance information and, on many occasions (in the case of an automobile accident), a diagram of the accident scene. The report generally has witness information, such as names and addresses so that we can speak to witnesses and take statements, if there are none contained within the police report. If there is substantial personal injury involved, I will also request copies of the medical records to review before meeting with the client again to discuss the case. It can take months to compile and review all of the information in a complex personal injury case, especially in cases in which the injured party has been admitted to a hospital for several weeks.

In trying to determine if my potential client has a claim, I must first consider factors such as, "Did the injured party have a pre-existing injury that was aggravated by this injury?" or, "Has the doctor made a prognosis for the client's short-term and long-term medical needs?" The medical prognosis has a huge impact on the case as I cannot begin to settle the claim until I know what the medical outlook for the client is.

Unfortunately, I have seen lawyers make the mistake of settling claims too early because their clients had medical bills to pay and seemed to be better. The clients then released all claims against the other party only to discover that they needed another surgery, or they were not getting any better. However, at that time it was too late for the attorney to do anything because the clients had already signed a full release and settled the claim. In order to avoid this, the process of investigation sometimes needs to be a long one. I do not believe in jumping in, signing a retainer agreement, moving for a quick settlement, and then leaving clients in an unacceptable position.

Once I have completed the investigation process, I meet with the client to ask any questions that I might have regarding the information discovered during the course of the investigation. I can then proceed with diagnosing the legal issues involved. Whether I am dealing with a personal injury case, commercial litigation case or another type of claim, each situation has three main points to consider. The first point is liability. By the time I have completed my investigation, I have a fairly good idea of my chances of proving that the other party was liable for my client's injuries. In Texas, it is very important to prove that the other party was primarily liable for the injuries sustained. If the injured party is 50% liable or more for his own injuries, he is not able to recover damages from the other party. Therefore, I have to make sure that I am fairly comfortable that, during the ensuing trial, the jury is going to decide that the other party was more responsible for the accident than my client was. For example, if there are no witnesses to an automobile accident and both parties claim they had the green light while the other driver had the red light, it comes down to who the jury will believe. If the jury believes that both parties were equally at fault, then my client does not recover any damages.

The second point to consider in a personal injury case is damages. This is the reason for performing a thorough investigation at the very beginning. An attorney must be patient and wait to get all of the medical records and billing records to determine what the client has suffered as a result of the accident. This is much easier than determining what the future medical bills may be and the amount of damages the client may incur going forward. This is a large component of the damages that we need to assess in order to determine the value of the personal injury claim.

The third point to consider is collectability. Typically, my cases involve a third party that is insured, therefore, collectability is not an issue. However, there have been cases in which a private party is involved who is not insured, or a business is involved that may be self-insured. In these cases, I must make a determination as to whether my client is likely to be able to collect damages in the event that I do win the case. If we receive a large monetary judgment but cannot collect any money from the defendant, then we have just wasted two years. It is extremely difficult in Texas, and in a number of other states, to collect a judgment against an individual because property laws provide a tremendous amount of equity in property that is exempt from judgment creditors. In most states, this includes the homestead, qualified retirement accounts, some liquid assets and personal property. Once the exempt assets are removed, $10,000 of a $1 million judgment is often all that is left, and the proposition of taking on the case becomes less attractive. An attorney must examine collectability very carefully when an insurance company is not involved on behalf of the defendant. This is one of the reasons that these types of cases are so complex. A complete investigation must be conducted to determine liability, the value of the damages in question and the collectability of those damages in order to ensure that it is worth both the client's and the attorney's time to proceed with a case.

Clients are often perplexed when I begin discussing the complexities of a case, including the fact that there may be liens involved, and there may be contribution or indemnity claims from their own health insurance company. If my client suffers a traumatic head injury that results in a hospital stay of six weeks, health insurance will probably pay the $300,000 medical bill. However, when we settle the case, the health insurance company will expect to be reimbursed for every dollar it paid for medical care that resulted from injuries sustained in the accident. This is an example of how a personal injury case continues to be complex even after a settlement has been reached and how an attorney must anticipate these issues even before the case has been settled. There is still a tremendous amount of work involved in resolving these types of issues after the settlement has been received. I explain to my clients that part of the service we are providing is obtaining a settlement, but we will also deal with issues, such as liens, subrogation rights, contribution claims, and indemnity claims, after the case has been settled.

For example, if the hospital places a lien against my client for medical bills, I cannot disburse any settlement funds until that lien is resolved. As the attorney, I can be susceptible to criminal penalties if I disburse the funds without resolving the lien. I will usually deal with a comptroller or CFO in the accounting office or even someone higher in management if the dollar amount is substantial. I negotiate to pay them the least amount per dollar so that I retain as much money for my client as possible. Sometimes, that can be as low as 25 cents per dollar or as high as 85 cents per dollar. If a health insurance company has paid medical bills on behalf of the client, there may be a contractual obligation for the client to reimburse the health insurance company from the proceeds of the settlement. If that is the case, then I must also negotiate with the health insurance company to settle the reimbursement claim. The client cannot receive any of the settlement proceeds until all of these issues have been resolved.

When an attorney first meets with a client, the client often has no idea what is involved with regards to preparing the case or the matters that must be resolved after the case is settled. It is evident from what I have described that navigating a personal injury claim can be quite complex. Because the client is unaware of the complexities of the personal injury case, the attorney would be doing a disservice to his client and his client would likely be unhappy if the attorney did not take each component of this very complex equation seriously. I never want to work for two or three years to resolve a claim only to have a client complain about the results at the end of the case. I have found that it reduces any bad feelings at the end of a case if I explain the very detailed nature of the process from the very beginning.

YOUR HEALTH INSURANCE COMPANY WANTS YOUR MONEY

I would like to take some time to discuss subrogation rights in more detail. Most people who have health insurance through their employer probably do not realize that they actually have a contract with the health insurance company. The health insurance company has various obligations under the contract as does the insured. It is frustrating for me and for my client, when we are six months or more into a personal injury case, to receive a letter from the client's health insurance company, putting us on notice that we must not, under any circumstances, distribute any funds related to the third party claim without first contacting the company to determine what the company's reimbursement claim will be. To me, there is an inherent unfairness in this because the insurance company seeks reimbursement for providing medical care when the injured person has suffered damages as a result of an injury that is not the person's fault. The insured may have been paying health insurance premiums for 20 years without ever requiring more than routine healthcare.

Therefore, my first question to the health insurance company's representative when the issue of reimbursement is raised is, "Are you going to refund the premiums that my client has paid for the last 20 years? Because now you want to be reimbursed for the one claim this person has made during those 20 years. The insured has been faithfully paying premiums to you without any benefit."

In most cases, I am not actually dealing with the health insurance company but a company that has been hired to collect the claim. When I receive the letter, usually from the sub-contracted company, I tell my clients that these people will badger us until the matter is resolved. However, I advise my client to proceed to settle the case, pay my fee and give them the money they are entitled to receive. That is because this is a contractual issue, not a lien, which may result in criminal liability if we do not resolve the issue prior to distributing the settlement proceeds. If the health insurance company continues to seek reimbursement, we have an advantage because we have the money, and we can negotiate with the health insurance company for a lower amount. Unfortunately, however, I have noticed a trend in which the collection agencies for the health insurance companies have become more aggressive. Because of this, I now deal with the issue from the beginning of the case. I work with the companies to determine the exact amount that is owed to the health insurance company as we are preparing to settle the case. It helps me to evaluate the case and to inform my client so that he will know about how much to expect as a settlement and that he must pay some of that back to his health insurance company.

TEXTING WHILE DRIVING

Changing subjects, I want to discuss the texting while driving issue as this is an evolving issue of law that concerns everyone. This is certainly a subject for most adults but especially for parents of the junior high and high school students who are beginning to drive or who are in the car with other young adults. Children today communicate by text even more than they talk on the telephone and, unfortunately, this often occurs while they are driving a vehicle. The National Safety Council recently released statistics showing that texting while driving causes 1,600,000 accidents each year. It expects that this number will continue to rise because of the increased use of cell phones in our country. Approximately 330,000 people each year are injured as a result of accidents in which the driver is texting. The

Council estimates that 11 teenagers die each day in texting while driving accidents across the country.

The National Highway Transportation and Safety Administration states that texting while driving makes drivers 23 times more likely to cause an accident. Insurance companies and other organizations are doing a fairly good job of educating all of us on the dangers of texting while driving. I read a statistic that said the average time it takes to read a text is about four to five seconds. Therefore, if someone is traveling at 45 mph and driving while texting, this driver will have traveled the length of a football field without having eyes on the road. We are seeing an increase in the commercial warnings about the dangers of texting while driving, which I think is good. Unfortunately, I have experienced an increase in the number of telephone calls my office is receiving that relate to devastating injuries sustained from texting while driving accidents, so I am trying to stay in front of the laws here in Texas that relate to this issue. At this time in Texas, if people are caught texting while driving, they receive citations. In some jurisdictions, the penalties are a lot more significant if someone is driving while texting in a school zone. I believe most jurisdictions have adopted—or at least drafted—a criminal statute that takes into account someone who is texting while driving in a school zone.

One case in particular comes from the Superior Court in New Jersey entitled Kubert vs. Best et al, and Shannon Colonna. Two people were texting each other—one was driving and one was at her home—when the driver caused an accident which resulted in serious injury to another party. The injured person sued the driver for damages but also sued the person whom the driver was texting. The case went to trial and was appealed until it reached the New Jersey Superior Court. The final opinion is a little alarming to those of us who text from anywhere other than a vehicle because, in a vehicle, we have the choice of texting knowing that we are driving and assuming the risk if we choose to text while driving. The New Jersey Superior Court held that if a person sends a text to someone, knowing the person is driving a vehicle, or responds to a text from someone knowing the person is driving, the non-driving individual, as well as the driver of the vehicle, can be held liable for any accident caused by the driver due to texting with the person. In this specific case, the sender of the text was not held liable because there was no evidence in the record that she had known that the person to whom she had sent the text was driving. However, the court said if there had been sufficient evidence to prove that she had known, then the non-driving sender of the text could have been held jointly responsible. I think that is the way this issue is going to proceed through our courts. I believe there are already other courts in various states across the country that are deciding to undertake this very approach to the issue. I am telling my clients, my friends, and my family members that this is something they should be aware of when they are texting other people.

Whether we are lawyers, teachers, insurance adjusters, or concerned parents, I think we can all agree that something must be done to curtail the carnage that is taking place on our highways from what appears to be the innocent act of looking over for a few seconds to read a text. I am torn on this issue. On one hand, as a concerned father and citizen, I think it is a good thing to expand the scope of liability if it will prevent individuals from texting people who they know are driving, due to their being scared of accountability in a trial. On the other hand, there is the matter of a civil liberties argument that government is getting too big, and it is an expansion that is just unreasonable. I can see this side of the argument also. Either way, it is a fascinating subject that is now being addressed across the country. Even though Texas may be one of the last states to adopt this ruling, as our courts are very conservative, I believe in the next five to ten years there will be a statute in every state that will penalize someone who knowingly sends a text to someone who is driving. If that text results in an accident, the sender will be liable, with the driver, for damages sustained in the accident. It will also be interesting to see how insurance companies react to this as they usually stay ahead of these issues. We may see policy exclusions for this type of issue to keep insurance companies from paying on these claims. I believe that texting while driving is an issue that should be important to all of us, and we should all be interested in where the law is heading as we could be held liable even though we were not in the vehicle at the time of an accident.

DRUNK DRIVING PERSONAL INJURY ACCIDENTS

Moving forward, I would like to talk a little bit about drunk driving accidents. When clients who have been injured by a drunk driver call me, they are often fearful that the insurance company will deny them the claim because the insurance policy had some type of exclusion for driving under the influence. However, this is typically not the case. I enjoy drunk driving cases, not because someone has been injured, but because I can use my experience as a criminal prosecutor when trying drunk driving cases. Working for four years in Houston as a prosecutor, I became very experienced in these types of cases; certainly more so than a normal attorney would be. There is a good bit of science involved in a drunk driving case. In Texas, in order to be adjudicated for a DWI, the attorney must prove that the person who was driving lost the normal use of their mental or physical faculties as a result of the introduction of alcohol or drugs into their system and that was the reason the accident occurred.

Unfortunately, there are many drunk driving accidents that result in a fatality to another party, but the drunk driver comes away unscathed. In discussing this with several physicians and medical experts, I have learned that the reason for this phenomenon could be that intoxication causes a person to be in a relaxed state. Normally, in an accident, the natural reaction of the occupants of the car is to tense up and become stiff in anticipation of the impending impact. When the human body is in this state, the impact can be devastating to its integrity and structure. However, when a person is drunk, the body is essentially limp. Therefore, when a drunk person is in an accident, the body can absorb the impact much more easily than when it is tense and rigid. I am always amazed when I view accident pictures and discover that the other party was killed but the drunk driver did not have any broken bones or even a concussion.

Clients come to my office with a drunk driving case assuming that they only have a claim against the drunk driver. However, I always look at an extra layer in these cases. Most of the time, when people are on the highway, especially at night, and they have had too much to drink; they are typically not coming from their home. People may drink at home, but they usually stay at home after they drink. Generally, people who are driving while drunk are coming from a commercial establishment, such as a sports bar, a restaurant, or a hotel. My clients never consider that they might have a claim against the establishment that served the drunk driver. Texas and, I believe, most other states, has a course of action called a dram shop claim. These statutes date back to long ago when states sought to punish people who served alcohol to a customer when it was obvious that the individual had already drunk too much.

For example, a person goes to a bar. He has eight shots of liquor and is then stumbling around, is vomiting, or has slurred speech. If the bar continues to serve him alcohol when he is obviously drunk, and then he gets into his car and causes an accident that injures or kills another person, the drunk driver is held liable but so is the bar that served him the alcohol. However, these dram shop cases are very complicated.

From my perspective, the commercial enterprises have done a fairly good job of watering down what the law used to be like in Texas. Currently, if a customer goes into a bar and he has too much to drink, and it is obvious that he has had too much to drink from the server's perspective (based on the server's training and experience), and that person gets into a car accident and injures someone, then the bar could be liable. However, under Texas law, there is what is called a safe harbor provision, which means that if the commercial establishment has a policy that requires its servers to attend Texas Alcohol and Beverage Commission-certified courses on serving alcohol, and if it can prove that its employee actually went to the certified courses, then the establishment can be absolved of any liability. All that is left to pursue is the individual liability against the server. There is no vicarious liability against the owner of the bar. This means that there is basically no dram shop claim except against a server who probably does not have the means to pay a monetary judgment. The attorney therefore has a collectability issue. So, sometimes, it reverts back to the fact that the only person being held responsible for the accident is the actual drunk driver himself.

There have been a number of cases, with a wild variety of scenarios, in which commercial establishments have been held liable. For example, a bar had a policy that all servers must attend TABC-certified courses, but the bar did not actually make the servers attend the courses or verify that the servers had attended the courses. If the bar disregards its own policy, the attorney may be able to hold it liable in that case. Another example would be a bar that does make its servers attend TABC-certified courses and does verify that all servers attend the courses to make sure servers learn the signs of intoxication and how not to over-serve people. However, the bar has promotions on Friday nights of "Buy one shot, get one shot free" or "$0.99 margaritas." That type of promotion is a direct contradiction to the policy of teaching servers not to over-serve people by encouraging people to get drunk for less money. So, sometimes, the attorney can get the claim in that way.

People are often surprised to learn that a drunk driver may have a case against the bar under a dram shop case. Those cases are a little bit tougher to prevail in. For example, I go into a bar, and it is so obvious that I am intoxicated that I have lost the normal use of my mental and physical faculties, but the bartender keeps serving me in the name of getting a few extra dollars. If I fall over chairs on the way out and wrap my car around a tree when I leave the bar, then I have a cause of action against the bar. However, the attorney must overcome the issue of comparative fault and who is more responsible. Am I more responsible for drinking too much? Or is the bar more responsible? Who, at some point, should have acknowledged that I have had too much yet did not stop serving me? I do not mean to make it sound as if dram shop cases are easy because they are very difficult and complex. Because of the safe harbor provision and the complexity of the issues involved, clients really need a lawyer that has experience in that type of law in order to have a decent chance of establishing liability against a commercial establishment when there is a drunk driving accident.

Drunk driving cases require a tremendous amount of investigation because drunk drivers rarely remember where they were because they may have gotten a concussion or may have sustained other injuries in the accident. The attorney needs to piece together what happened prior to the accident. Sometimes, social media, text messages, and telephone records are used to establish where clients were and whom they talked to during that time. If the attorney can determine where the clients were when they placed a call or sent a text, the attorney can send a letter to that establishment requesting that its management preserve any videotape from that time period. The attorney can then begin interviewing witnesses and start to develop a case. There is so much involved in any personal injury case, from an investigation standpoint, and attorneys cannot afford to gloss over any part of the investigation, or they may miss something important. They must be willing to play the role of investigator or have a private investigator uncover the relevant facts.

Drunk driving cases are just like texting while driving cases. They both seem to be increasing in number each year even though we have a tremendous amount of education about the dangers of both. I guess because there are so many bars and establishments that serve alcohol, more and more people are getting hurt and killed each year on the roads by drunk drivers. Drunk driving is certainly an area of law that brings me many clients each year.

(This content should be used for informational purposes only. It does not create an attorney-client relationship with any reader

and should not be construed as legal advice. If you need legal advice, please contact an attorney in your community who can assess the specifics of your situation.)

6

I LOVE THAT I CAN HELP PEOPLE INJURED IN AN ACCIDENT

by James Heiting, Esq.

James Heiting, Esq.
Heiting & Irwin
Riverside, California

James Heiting is Past President of the State Bar of California (2005-2006), and served on the State Bar Board of Governors (2002-2006). He is or has been a member of multiple federal and state litigation, ethics, and trial associations, is admitted to practice law before all state and federal courts in California, the United States Court of Federal Claims, and the California and United States Supreme Courts. He also has served as president of a variety of legal organizations and co-founded an organization to train younger or less experienced lawyers.

136

The managing partner of Heiting and Irwin, a Professional Law Corporation, he has a very active practice in prosecuting and defending wrongful death, personal injury and medical malpractice matters.

I LOVE THAT I CAN HELP PEOPLE INJURED IN AN ACCIDENT

The young man, barely 18 years old and a senior in a small farm community's high school, dove into the canal at the swimming hole where kids have been swimming and diving for years. Only this time, when he surfaced, his friends noticed that he seemed limp and rolled in the current like a rag doll. In fact, he had broken his neck when he dove, hitting what we believe was a submerged cement block, placed at that point under the surface of the water and hidden from view, without warning, by the water district - the water district that knew kids floated down that canal and partied at that spot, swimming and diving there while water district employees were nearby going about their business.

That young man was rendered a quadriplegic, paralyzed from the neck down. A firm that claimed to do personal injury cases "investigated" the accident and rejected any potential case. The family came to us, and we checked records, sent people to the community, interviewed what seemed like the entire population from the high school, and uncovered the facts that the prior law firm had missed. We took the case, filed in court, and litigated it to a very successful conclusion, giving that young man the best possible future he could have under the circumstances.

I love that I can help people and that I can be an instrument of change in this world. I became a lawyer because my family placed our entire future in the hands of a lawyer when I was a young man, but that lawyer seemed preoccupied with other things, other cases, other interests, and he was a poor communicator, leaving us in the dark about what we felt was the most important thing happening in our lives. I was fearful and frustrated, and I made a decision to become a lawyer, vowing to do a better job and to make a difference, and I have been gratified by the results.

MAKING A DIFFERENCE

We have been able to change many things and practices that really have made a difference. For example, the cases we have taken on have:

- made streets safer for the traveling public, avoiding future deadly accidents by forcing changes in dangerous conditions or roadway design and use;
- changed the way spinal surgeries are done to avoid resulting paralysis;
- changed how experiments are done in high school science labs and what safety equipment should be utilized, avoiding chemical and other burns, blindness, and devastating injuries to students;
- caused changes to the way the water district does its job;
- caused gas companies and public utilities to protect high-pressure gas lines from possible impacts that resulted in explosions, terrible burns, and death;
- caused changes in automotive battery maintenance and safety practices;

- improved mental health practices and procedures in psychiatric hospitals;
- created railroad protection for small children in the communities through which the train travels;
- forced better practices of micro-surgery and operations involving the brain;
- resulted in transportation safety methods (including trains, buses, and other forms of public transportation);
- improved safety practices of trucking companies and drivers of semi-truck/trailer rigs;
- created focus on faulty "pop-off" valves on propane tanks used in barbecuing; and
- the list goes on and on.

Lawsuits and claims are not a walk in the park by any means, and many elements included in a lawsuit must be considered throughout the whole process. Turning the matter over to a lawyer doesn't mean that a check will appear the very next week. When I accept the responsibility of taking a case, I strongly feel that I am also taking a responsibility for part of that person's life. It's my job as their attorney to work hard to get the best possible result, and keep them updated throughout the process. *This is their life.* It is a pivotal point that will affect their future. Because we understand this, our attorneys spend a great deal of time and put forth a great deal of effort getting to know our clients and making them part of our legal family.

With regard to a client's expectations, we see concern, worry, and fear when they first come in. What will the future hold? How has my life changed? Will it ever be okay again? Will we lose everything? Is there help for us? By the time they leave our first consultation, we want to see hope and relief. Especially in serious injury cases, we see the hope that there will be enough money to pay the mortgage, put food on the table, or even buy a Little League uniform for a child. We see their relief when the clients realize they have a champion who cares, who will shoulder their burdens, who will take up their cause. It is an extremely dark and difficult time when the wage earner, the provider for the family, the family's "rock," is injured or killed. We work very hard to help and to find and develop resources for them.

We become invested in our clients' lives and work hard to understand and resolve their unique problems and difficulties. Basically, we want to become "part of the family" and truly understand the dreams, hopes, aspirations, and expectations that were shattered when they suffered serious injuries or the loss of a loved one, their belief system(s), social network(s), and how the accident has affected and dramatically changed their lives.

In a truck accident case, a family lost their father and husband. This man was an undocumented worker from Mexico, but he and his family had resided in the United States for almost 30 years. He was still considered an "illegal," without papers, but he worked hard, had all legal deductions taken from his pay, had insurance on his car, and filed income taxes, just as he was supposed to do. He paid in to Social Security, even though he and his family might not ever be able to take advantage of his contributions.

As we explored the case, and once we got involved with the family and saw how this man was involved in his community as a whole (not just the Mexican-American community), we could see why we needed to be involved in this case. He and his wife studied and spoke fluent English and worked hard to be good members of the community. They had taken steps to become "legal" and were working toward citizenship. His children were born in the United States and were legal citizens. He coached in the soccer leagues, sang in and put on karaoke events, and had fun with his children and the neighborhood kids. He was admired as a coach and as a religious leader in his church. In his local community, he was as solid a man as you would ever want to meet. His family revolved around him. He was central not only to their lives, but also to the lives of their cousins, aunts, uncles, and other people who were close to their family. They relied on him for leadership and much, much more. Once a jury got to know the family, they could understand the dynamics and share the love and admiration the family had for him.

Neglecting to understand the entire stories of human beings who suffer these tragedies is a disservice to clients, but many lawyers just do not take the time or do not have the interest, in my opinion, to do so, and this is at the expense of the clients. As we started to recognize the damage and the extent of the loss that was suffered by this family — by his two sons, his wife, and the whole community — we could realistically prepare a case that a jury could appreciate.

Serious injuries (i.e., brain damage, scarring and disfigurement, physical impairments, broken bones, paralysis, death, burns, need for surgery, etc.) have long-lasting effects on the entire family that change the courses of their lives. Serious injury cases are handled quite differently than whiplash or minor injury cases, whether the serious injury is due to medical malpractice, products liability, premises liability, wrongful death, a plane, train, bus or automobile accident, a truck accident, a construction accident, or some other type of accident. As the family's attorney, I view my job as a commitment to get that family back to the point where they are as whole as possible, and get them enough money so that they can realize their dreams and aspirations.

Some of our most tragic cases are burn injury cases. Burns cause disfigurement, or the loss of use of a limb or other body parts, and these cases cause great emotional as well as physical pain. As attorneys, we represent our clients to obtain a fair and just settlement. However, I believe we also have a duty to use our resources to find our clients the best doctors and burn clinics so that they get the best treatment available and make the best recovery possible. Whether they suffer from chemical burns, electrical burns, burns from a fire, or other burns, people who suffer burn injuries will always have scars, both emotionally and physically. Our job is to make a difference in their lives, to improve their circumstances, and to give them new opportunities and dreams.

And this practice is true concerning all serious injuries. We keep in contact with our clients to make sure they are doing well long after their cases have ended. I keep in touch with clients and families from over 30 years ago that I have represented in serious personal injury and wrongful death cases. It is a joy to see them doing well as a result of our efforts and being able to go on with their lives after living through such horrific events.

How Do I Find A Good Attorney?

When searching for a good personal injury attorney, a client should consider the successes and reputation of the attorney(s). What is the attitude of the attorney? What are the factors to consider to have good, satisfactory access, a ready ability to talk to the lawyer, and get answers to questions? Is it important to retain counsel whose offices are local or fairly local to the client's residence or the court district?

Without question, look for someone who is highly rated by their clients and by other attorneys and judges. Attorney ratings can be found on services such as "AVVO" or "Martindale-Hubbell." Our firm is rated 10 out of 10 or *"SUPERB"* by AVVO, and retains the *"PREEMINENT"* rating by Martindale-Hubbell, each the highest rating that any firm or lawyer can receive. This is the result of years of practice with the highest rating in legal ability and ethical standards.

Review the firm's ratings. Check the personal injury experience level of the firm and the attorneys. Avoid hiring a fly-by-night attorney, or an attorney who handles mostly contract or other cases but will take on your personal injury case "as a favor" or to make a quick dollar. Go to an attorney who works in this field every hour of every day. Go to attorneys who are solely dedicated to handling personal injury cases and wrongful death cases. Finally, look to attorneys who are involved in the community where they practice and are respected for their professional achievements by the legal community. You will want to have access to someone you can trust and whom the community trusts.

WHAT ABOUT FEES?

Almost all personal injury cases are based on a ***contingency fee***, which means that the attorney is not paid until and unless the client is paid. Whether money is recovered by way of a settlement or at trial, the lawyer is not paid anything until and unless the client receives money. The attorney's fee would then be a percentage of the client's recovery amount. Our firm usually charges rates depending on the case and the state of the litigation. As we get closer to trial, more time, money, and effort are involved, and the fees will bump up a bit. There could be several levels of fees. For example, a certain percentage might be appropriate at the time of settling the case *before litigation*, or if settling a case *prior to mediation* attempts or prior to *trial preparation*, or at *trial*, or upon *judgment*, and then a final level for *after-trial* work. In *medical malpractice* cases, a fee schedule is set by law. This is the only type of personal injury case in California (other than some specialized cases, such as in Veteran's Administration cases) that has a fee schedule set by law. It is still based on a contingency fee, so the client does not pay unless and until the lawyer recovers a monetary amount for the client. In cases involving *injuries to a child*, the court will review the fees to ensure that the lawyer fees are reasonable.

Contingency fees work well for both the client and the attorney. The attorney is taking a risk, but also has the opportunity to share in a successful award, while the client benefits by excellent representation without paying high hourly rates for these very accomplished lawyers or risking up-front attorney's fees and costs in a case that might not be successful. This allows everyone to have access to the court system and very experienced, excellent representation, regardless of income level at the time of the accident (and the attorney assumes all risk of not recovering any fees, even if hundreds of hours have gone into the case). It is a risk-free method for the clients to have high-powered lawyers on their side through each step of the process.

WHY NOT HANDLE THE CASE MYSELF?

Personal injury cases often come down to an individual fighting a huge corporation or insurance company. Individuals who have been injured or lost a loved one due to negligence, carelessness, or the reckless act of another party are going up against an insurance company, business, or large corporation with multimillions — sometimes billions — of dollars in resources. It takes a dedicated, experienced personal injury attorney to invade and pierce that armor. We train, we study, we prepare. We relish the battle.

Anyone who has lost a loved one or who has been seriously or significantly injured should be represented by an experienced personal injury attorney. Consider the number of attorneys on the other side of a personal injury case, representing insurance companies and corporations. Then consider the advantages to having a trained and experienced warrior in your corner to do battle and carry your case to victory. When the benefits and advantages of having a lawyer compared to not having a lawyer (i.e., the other side taking advantage of you) are experienced, you will certainly want to have an attorney and not go into that battle unprepared.

Insurance companies are in business for profit. They are not our friends when we make a claim. Any claim that is settled is only settled because settlement is better than litigation for the organization's bottom line. When you are considering whether or not to hire a personal injury attorney, remember this: an insurance company employs hundreds and hundreds of lawyers to make sure that the claims are paid out at the lowest possible level, or not paid at all. From the very beginning, you are in an adversarial relationship with the insurance company (even your own). The insurance adjuster's job is to try to get you to settle that case at the lowest possible amount to minimize the impact to the company's profit margin. Imagine a David and Goliath picture, with David matched against a team of giants. David needs the slingshot (a good, experienced, tough lawyer) and the best and most effective ammunition (good marshaling of evidence and witnesses) to successfully take on these corporate giants.

WHAT CAN I EXPECT?

During our initial consultation, I want to get acquainted with the client(s) and have them get to know us. I explain the history of our firm and attorneys and our commitment to our clients, the law, and the community. And we discuss the case. This process could take up to a few hours, depending on the complexity of the matter and what may be necessary. Significant case factors are reviewed, including injuries, medical history and needs, the details of the accident or incident, and post-accident impacts and lifestyle changes. We will also explore what to expect as the claim progresses.

We handle a variety of wrongful death and personal injury cases: defects in property, defective products, the crash-worthiness of vehicles, children who have been sexually abused and molested, medical malpractice, birth injuries, brain injuries, burns, paralysis, nursing home neglect, electrocution, explosions, injuries at school, accidents involving transportation (plane, train, bus, taxi), construction, job-related, and *many* others. But no matter what type of case it may be, the initial process is fairly similar: we get to know the people who will be our clients, discuss the relevant details of the case, and get moving on giving them the best possible representation they could get.

In the trucking case we talked about, we investigated everything from every angle to develop a strong case surrounding an 18-wheeler and the semi-truck driver's inattention to her job, even to the extent that facts emerging during the course of the investigation eventually led to her pleading guilty to manslaughter. And we were able to get a very good award for the family. Unfortunately, no dollar amount can ever replace their husband/father; however, that money will provide support, schooling, and education for his children. And it will allow his wife to be independent of the need to turn to others for support. One of his sons wants to be a professional in the medical field, and his other son wants to be a "master" in food preparation. They will be able to pursue the dreams that they would have pursued with their father, even to a greater extent than was possible before, even though he is gone. It is deeply satisfying to see a family's lives start to blossom again after we achieve a successful result for them. This family will never forget their father and husband, and they will carry him with them. We were able to see to it that he was able to provide for them, even in death.

WHAT ABOUT OTHER TYPES OF CASES?

The concept of liability for damages in our country dates back to our founding fathers and our Constitution. The person who causes an injury has the responsibility to make the injured individual "whole" again. That is the theory behind the personal injury case. We handle most types of cases that fit this description. In this short chapter, we have talked about some types of cases we handle. You might be interested in learning about some of the factors involved in some of our other cases.

Construction accidents usually carry two possible aspects: *workers' compensation* and *third party liability* (a claim against someone other than the employer). For example, let's say the client is working on a construction site where there are subcontractors such as a plumber, carpenter, or electrician, the client gets hurt while working for one of those subcontractors, but due to the negligence of one of the other subcontractors. Along with the right to a workers' compensation claim, the client also has the right to bring an additional claim against the subcontractor who caused the injury, with the possibility of better and more extensive recovery of damages than simply under workers' compensation. Workers' compensation is not intended to make the client "whole."

In order to handle a third party case like this, we think it helps to understand the construction industry as thoroughly as possible. Our attorneys have been members of several unions prior to becoming lawyers, including the Carpenters, Teamsters, Electricians, Plumbers and Pipefitters, and Ironworkers. With actual experience working in the construction industry and an understanding of unions and trades, we use our knowledge to give our clients an advantage.

Boating accidents tend to be very tragic. Deaths and very serious injuries occur when boats run into each other due to driver inattention, going the wrong way on the water, or a driver paying attention to a skier when they should be watching where they are driving. They can occur due to faulty maintenance or product failure. Skiers can be run down or run over by a boat, and very serious injuries can be caused by the propeller, resulting in loss of limbs, scarring, or incapacity. Inattention and horseplay can be devastating.

148

Very similar driving rules apply to boats as to vehicles. These include *drunk driving* laws. With drunk driving (whether in a boat or a vehicle), it's good for all people to understand that defendants cannot get relief of their responsibility in a drunk driving case by *filing for bankruptcy*. In some personal injury cases, the defendant may be able to escape some of the liability and the payment of damages by filing for bankruptcy; however, *in drunk driving* cases, including boating cases, the *defendant is not permitted to escape liability through bankruptcy*.

Premises liability cases (something involving the property causing injury) can be from garden variety slip and falls to any imaginable (and many times deadly) conditions of property. We handled one unusual case in which a woman in a convertible was driving down a driveway out in the country. There was a small, almost invisible wire strung as a "gate" across the driveway. As the wire came over the windshield, the "gate" acted like a bow with the wire as string, and the wire stretched tighter and tighter. When it came over the windshield it snapped down and hit the woman in the forehead. She was scalped and disfigured, and she lost an eye and her sense of smell — it was very tragic. The landowners' insurance company and the owner blamed the driver for the accident, even though there was no way to see this wire strung across the driveway between the two posts! We won that case after a lengthy trial and were able to recover a very good amount of money for our client.

Product liability cases deal with all types of defective products — for example, an exploding battery. In one such case, an insurance agent was working on his car to replace the battery when the battery unexpectedly exploded. His left eye was displaced, and he lost sight in that eye. After extensive discovery and litigation, and hiring the right experts and performing tests, we were able to determine that the battery should not have exploded under those conditions and why it did explode (and how to prevent such accidents in the future). The young man in this case was an innocent victim, doing everything correctly, but still he suffered devastating injuries. We were able to get him a settlement that has paid him an annuity for the rest of his life, and were able to give him back lost opportunity and a chance at a happy and productive future.

Devices for hip and knee replacements, spinal apparatus (including plates, pins, screws, cages, and rods), electrical lamps, cords and motors, tires, reproductive products, implants, seatbelts, gas tanks, air bags, barbecues, children's float aids, monitoring methods (heart, blood pressure, sugar, GPS, etc.), protective shields and designs, warning systems, fire and smoke detectors, heaters, baby cribs, blinds and window coverings, brakes, steering, filtering systems, health aids, vitamins and medicines, asbestos, and about every product type you can imagine — even popcorn butter — have had defects or defective components that caused injury or death. These products are safer because of the attention given them after they have caused mayhem and the companies are forced to make changes through lawsuits.

Medical malpractice is another type of personal injury case, but a type that requires even greater study, experience, and expertise. Medical malpractice cases require experts on both sides. We must prove that the doctor, hospital, or medical practitioner had a certain standard of care that they should have met but failed to meet in the care of the patient, which failure led to that person's injury. Experts in a medical malpractice case must testify as to the standard of care involved (whether the medical provider was negligent) and how that standard of care was breached.

A typical jury does not have the expertise to determine if a medical standard of care was met or breached, let alone to review medical records and determine what really happened. The initial impression may simply be that what happened should not have happened. "This should not have happened. This 18-year-old, otherwise completely healthy boy, should not have died." Even with the best experts, a medical malpractice case is like a puzzle that we have to put together — we must determine what happened, why it happened, and whether or not it meets the standard of care, and the doctors involved don't always want to help put together the pieces.

Each side has its experts. The plaintiff's experts will say that the doctor had certain obligations which were not met, causing the injuries to the plaintiff. The defendant's experts will say that the doctor certainly met those obligations and did everything perfectly, or at least within the standard of care. The doctor did the best he/she possibly could. It is our burden to bring forth the truth and to expose the fallacies of a disingenuous defense. That is what medical malpractice is all about. The difficulty comes when a jury of 12 people who have little or no experience with medical standards, presented with experts from both sides contradicting each other, is trying to determine which side is right. The burden of proof lies with the plaintiff, but the law gives every advantage to the doctors. These are tough cases, but they can be won.

Medical malpractice cases are very complex, and they are very intense. The case will have great lawyers on both sides. I enjoy the challenge a great deal. However, it is also very frustrating that several states have *caps or limits on damages* in medical malpractice cases. In California, the highest limits are $250,000 in general damages for any injury or death, no matter how devastating or horrible! For example, a young girl — maybe your daughter — goes to the doctor for a benign cyst on her lower spine. After a couple of CT scans, the doctor recommends surgery and assures you that it is a simple procedure. However, your 8-year-old daughter goes in for the "simple surgery" and suffers brain damage during the procedure. She is now in constant pain and confusion. She seems to be fearful of anything and everything. Even you. She will require 24-hour care for the rest of her life (as much of it as possible from you and your spouse), but the case is limited to $250,000 in general damages for *all* of the loss, pain, and suffering. That is just ridiculous. It is my hope that the legislators will someday get the guts to do the right thing and raise the limits rather than bend to the wishes of the insurance companies, big businesses, and their campaign supporters. There has been no raise on the cap in California in decades.

On the other side of the coin, people suffer injuries because a doctor recommends a procedure but the *insurance company refuses to pay*. In some cases, people have serious medical conditions that require treatment like dialysis or chemotherapy, but the insurance company denies coverage or refuses to authorize the treatment. There are some remedies, but they may be totally unsatisfactory. They are unsatisfactory because the damage is done, and it takes a very long time to remedy the situation. There may, in fact, be no remedy left. In a *breach of contract* case or a *bad faith* case against an insurance company, there are damages to be proved for their failure to act reasonably and deal fairly with their insured. Sometimes, through the courts, the insurance company can be compelled to act in the right way, and a court order is issued requiring the insurance company to provide the necessary treatment. The problem, though, is that the damage may already be done, and the long-term effects on this person's life have occurred, or the person has now died. It really seems unsatisfactory to me to simply get money when the person has died or suffered long-term effects and the insurance company could have avoided this by treating their customer fairly, meeting their obligations, and paying for the medical treatment. Unfortunately, monetary awards become our only recourse for forcing insurance companies to act in a responsible manner — teaching them a lesson this time so that the next patient who needs care may receive it when it is needed.

SOME GENERAL THOUGHTS

Most of us drive, and *automobile insurance* policies are very important. I advise all of my clients (and everyone else who is willing to accept sound advice) to increase *underinsured and uninsured* motorist coverage to the highest possible level. The premiums are typically inexpensive compared to the amount of coverage received. Having this coverage can make a huge difference to you if you are involved in a serious automobile accident. If your injuries exceed the other person's policy limits, you can then turn to your own insurance company and recover what could have been recovered from the other person, had they carried a higher policy limit. It is very important that you do not decline this coverage (or carry policy limits lower than you can afford). If you don't have the additional coverage, your ability to recover damages may be severely limited.

Insurance companies will ask the injured party to make a *recorded statement* and sign *medical release forms*. While the insurance company will eventually need to know details about the injuries, along with getting copies of medical records, anyone with a potential personal injury claim should consult with an attorney prior to signing any forms or providing any statement to the insurance company. Insurance companies will always send a *blanket authorization* rather than just an authorization that is specific to your injury as they should. The company wants to obtain all of your medical records (which may include your previous pregnancies, your sprained ankle as a 6-year-old, your tonsillectomy, your STD, etc.). I am sure you get the picture. This is a terrible invasion of your privacy. It is important that access to client records is limited to make sure that insurance companies get what they need, but only what they need. A lawyer representing your interests can provide the insurance company with just the necessary medical records that are directly related to the injury in question. Good attorneys will ensure that any authorizations signed by the client(s) are limited to just those medical records related to the injury and the case at hand.

Regarding the signing of *consent forms*, every hospital procedure will require that the patient or patient representative sign a consent form granting permission to the hospital and staff to perform the proposed procedure. These consent forms are very general in nature and really do not review the actual risks of the procedure. Although a medical malpractice claim may include a lack of informed consent, or that the client was not informed of all the risks involved with the procedure, it would be best for the patient to demand to speak to the doctor and get all the details, ask questions, and really understand the risks he or she is facing. The doctor, though perhaps a bit put out by having to spend the time to go over this, will be more attuned to the risks and to the individual patient as another human being and not just another procedure leading to an insurance check.

Many businesses, and almost all medical facilities, may ask the customer to sign an *Arbitration Agreement*, which, basically, states that the person signing agrees that they waive any right to jury trial and must go to arbitration for any disputed claim. Sometimes the business or facility will refuse to treat or do business at all if the Arbitration Agreement is not signed. *Jury trials* are *important safeguards* to our rights in America. Sometimes the Arbitration Agreement can be voided, even after signed. Sometimes it is better not to do business with such places.

There are *alternatives* to going to court. Some individuals are reluctant to go forward with their case because they fear it will be necessary that they go to court and testify in front of a judge and jury. It is a very uncomfortable thought for them. Sometimes, we prefer to take the case before a jury if that will result in our client having an advantage in receiving the fair compensation they deserve. We make these decisions on a case-by-case basis. Having a jury trial is often the best way to go. However, *alternative dispute resolution (ADR)* methods are sometimes viable alternatives to taking a case to trial. *Arbitration and mediation* can be very effective tools to shorten litigation and permit the parties more control over the litigation and ultimate resolution of the case. The attorneys here at Heiting & Irwin have been very effective in mediations and arbitrations for a very long time. Several of our attorneys are certified mediators.

In Conclusion

I always keep in mind how I want to act; I put myself in my client's position, and I plan how to be most effective. I am always thinking of how to manage the system to the greatest advantage of my client. Hopefully, this chapter will help you to do the same.

Give me a call anytime. I look forward to talking to you.

Best wishes,
Jim Heiting
Former President, California State Bar

(This content should be used for informational purposes only. It does not create an attorney-client relationship with any reader and should not be construed as legal advice. If you need legal advice, please contact an attorney in your community who can assess the specifics of your situation.)

7

ONLY HIRE AN ATTORNEY THAT SPECIALIZES IN PERSONAL INJURY CASES

by James D. Hagelgans, Esq.

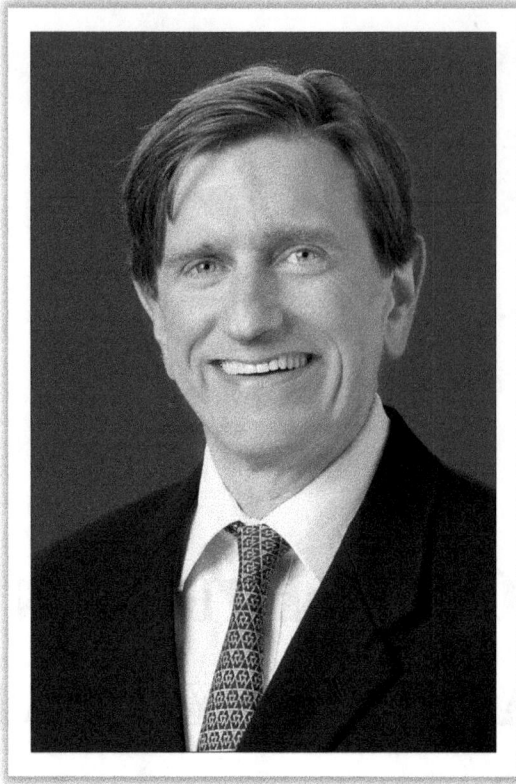

James D. Hagelgans, Esq.
Hagelgans & Veronis
Lancaster, Pennsylvania

Jim is a trial lawyer who has over 32 years of experience, in settling, and litigating auto accident claims, death cases and cases involving serious personal injuries.

He holds professional memberships with the American Trial Lawyers Association and the Pennsylvania Association for Justice. Jim is a certified member of the Million Dollar Advocates Forum, a group of lawyers, made up of less than 1%

of all attorneys in the United States, who have recovered settlements, awards and verdicts of $1,000,000 or more.

The Judges of Lancaster County have appointed Jim to serve as a Chairman of Civil Arbitration Panels (a lawyer who is appointed to act as a Judge, hear sworn testimony in civil cases and render decisions along with two other panel members).

ONLY HIRE AN ATTORNEY THAT SPECIALIZES IN PERSONAL INJURY CASES

When someone asks me why he or she should hire a personal injury attorney, my response is that it just makes sense to at least consult with a personal injury attorney to see if you even have a claim. Most personal injury attorneys offer a free consultation; therefore, it is just practical to take advantage of the free time offered by the attorney to find out if you have a claim, and what that claim might be worth. I strongly suggest that you meet with an attorney who specializes in personal injury cases rather than an attorney who handles a variety of cases such as family law, real estate, and probate law in addition to personal injury work. You need someone who limits his practice to personal injury cases due to their complex nature. Because a personal injury claim involves so many different issues, you want someone who has the experience with, and knowledge about handling personal injury cases to develop your claim and who will be able to protect your interests so that you can recover for all aspects and elements of your claim.

It is so important to have an attorney who limits his or her cases to personal injury claims, because you want someone who is going to stay on top of your case. You also want a personal injury attorney who will stay in constant contact with you as he develops the case to make sure that you are recovering. For example, there have been times when a client has been focused on an injury, thinking that it was the only one, only to find out later, after the pain began to subside, that he had other injuries he was not aware of at the time of the accident. These are just some of the things that can come up in a personal injury case. My advice: hire an experienced personal injury attorney who will stay on top of your case, will stay in constant contact with you, and will not assign your case to an associate or paralegal who does not have the experience necessary to fully develop a personal injury claim.

Unfortunately, anyone can be involved in an accident. Many of our clients never had a reason to hire an attorney before they were injured in an accident. Most clients are not able to work due to their injuries; therefore, they do not have the means to hire an attorney on an hourly basis. With a contingency fee, the client does not pay for our services until and unless we recover damages on his behalf. The benefit of the contingency fee agreement for the client is that he can afford to have a highly qualified personal injury attorney representing him and protecting his interests without worrying about paying the attorney until he receives money from a settlement. This means that anyone, no matter what his or her means, can afford to have quality representation. This is very important because on the other side, you have the insurance company and its attorneys with almost unlimited resources fighting to pay as little as possible for the claim. In order to prevail on your claim, your attorney must spend a lot of time working on your case. If you were charged by the hour, this could quickly become very expensive, and you would be paying most of your settlement in attorney's fees. Furthermore, most clients do not have the funds to pay in advance for experts or doctors to testify on their behalf, so it just makes sense for the attorney to bear the costs of the case and to be reimbursed from the settlement proceeds. Divorce attorneys, criminal attorneys, and business attorneys typically charge by the hour, but most personal injury attorneys work on a contingency fee basis. Of course, your personal injury attorney is going to work hard to get you the best possible settlement because the more money you receive, the more money he can earn. It is an efficient way to handle personal injury cases and is very beneficial to the clients as well as the attorneys. Clients receive representation from highly qualified attorneys and do not pay unless the attorney recovers damages on behalf of the client.

INSURANCE COMPANIES ARE NOT LOOKING OUT FOR YOUR BEST INTEREST

Speaking of insurance companies, most people do not realize that the insurance company is against them. They assume that the case is what it is, and that they really do not need a personal injury attorney to deal with the insurance company because facts are facts. As a matter of fact, I met with two individuals just recently who tried to deal with the insurance company on their own. They now have an attorney because they were not offered a fair and just settlement for their claim. The insurance company raised issues that were not really issues, and did not fully evaluate the claim. In one case, they claimed that the accident was not the reason that the woman needed major spinal surgery. However, the insurance company never requested the woman's medical records which proved that she never had treatment for her back before the accident occurred. She had never even considered or been referred for back surgery. Instead of looking into it, the insurance company raised a few alleged issues and offered her only a nominal settlement. The insurance company may tell you that they are looking out for you, but they are really a business, and they are looking out for their bottom line. Since their goal is to make a profit, they will always try to pay the lowest amount possible to settle a claim. That does not mean they are evil people, but they are just doing their jobs.

I believe the misunderstanding occurs when people believe that the insurance company is working for them. Whether it is an automobile accident claim, a slip and fall claim, or another type of personal injury claim, the insurance company is not working for you. It is working for the person who caused you to be injured. The insurance company is interested in paying you the lowest amount possible to settle your claim. Because of this, you definitely should always talk to an attorney whenever you have a personal injury claim. If for no other reason, you should talk to a reputable personal injury attorney to find out what your options are, because it should not cost you anything to discuss your case. Any honest, legitimate attorney will tell you if your case involves minimal damages or minimal insurance, and if you can handle the settlement on your own. However, those cases are few and far between in my practice. Most of the time, it is not so cut-and-dry, and you need an attorney who can develop the claim, determine who should pay the medical bills and loss of income and establish whether certain parties have a right to reimbursement from the proceeds of your settlement. It is very complicated, and frankly, it is getting more complicated all the time.

LANDMINES AND PITFALLS

Personal injury cases have many complexities that even some attorneys do not realize. I have been practicing for over 31 years, and I still see situations arise that I have never encountered before in other cases. I do know that having a personal injury attorney involved from the very beginning helps avoid some of the problems that can arise during a case. Unfortunately, some of my clients had to learn this the hard way. By the time they came to see me, they had not sought treatment for their injuries, and had just let things go along without the advice or counsel of a personal injury attorney. What they did not realize, is that a big gap in time between the accident and the treatment of injuries can be used against you during the case.

Seeking treatment from the right doctor is also very important. If you receive treatment from a doctor who does not specialize in that type of injury and you are misdiagnosed, or the doctor misses a diagnosis, it can be a problem. Not keeping proper documentation of every medical treatment and all bills that have been paid by you, an insurance company, or Medicare is an issue. Then we must try to determine who paid what and who has the right to be paid back out of the settlement proceeds.

If medical bills have been paid through public assistance, Medicare, a health insurance provider, or a worker's compensation provider, a personal injury attorney can negotiate with these providers to reduce the amount of money that must be paid back to them from the settlement proceeds. If you try to do this on your own, they will not reduce the bills, but an attorney can help.

We have people come to our office who think they had recovered completely from their injuries, sign a release and waiver of all known and unknown claims, and then realize they are not okay. At that point, there is nothing that we can do for them because they released the party from any further liability. There are just so many issues and so many different aspects of a personal injury claim where you need an attorney involved to make sure everything is taken care of properly.

To give you an idea of how we handle the initial contact for a potential personal injury claim in my office, let me walk you through an example. Before Internet use was as prevalent as it is today, people would call our office; however, we now receive contacts through the Internet and by email. I prefer to speak to the person by telephone, if possible, because it helps me to get a better feel for the situation. Contact through email can be difficult, as one question may lead to another, and it is much easier to do this when you are speaking with the person rather than sending emails back and forth. Nevertheless, the process is the same—we try to talk to the prospective client or the injured party as soon as possible, so we can inform him of the steps that need to be taken right away. Sometimes people will call and they really do not have a claim, so we can tell them that right away or explain the issues that we see based on what they have told us about the potential claim. We try to spend at least 30 minutes to an hour on the telephone with a potential client so that we can determine what, if anything, needs to be done immediately.

After the initial telephone consultation, we schedule an appointment with one of our attorneys to make sure that the clients are comfortable with us and want to proceed with retaining our office to represent them in their claim. If all parties are in agreement, we proceed to their signing of a written fee agreement in accordance with Pennsylvania law and an authorization so that we can obtain copies of their medical records and any other records we will need during their case. We have copies and the client has copies so that everyone understands the terms, even though the fee agreement is simple and straightforward. Once we have entered into an agreement to represent the client, we notify the insurance company of our representation so that the insurance company knows to contact our office and not our clients. Once there is an attorney involved, it protects you from having the insurance company representative contact you and possibly use anything you say out of context to hurt your case. After we notify the insurance company of our involvement, we will request copies of medical records and other records as we begin to work on the case, until we are in a position to try to resolve the claim or proceed to file a lawsuit. That is the basic process: telephone consultation, formal meeting, entering a written fee agreement, and then proceeding to develop the case toward settlement or a trial.

HEALTH INSURANCE COMPANIES SUBROGATION RIGHTS

On a different subject, I would like to discuss an issue that comes up in many cases and is becoming more and more complicated—health insurance subrogation rights. Prior to 1990, every driver in Pennsylvania was required to carry $10,000 medical coverage under his or her automobile insurance policy. In most cases, that was enough to cover the medical costs in an accident. However, in 1990, the amount was reduced from $10,000 in coverage to a minimum of $5,000 in coverage. Because of the lower amount, health insurance began paying the medical bills that exceeded the medical coverage under the automobile insurance policy. This is where subrogation rights began to play a role in personal injury settlements. Under a federal law, ERISA provided more and more companies or employers with the right of subrogation. What followed is that businesses across the country began sending letters to injured parties, putting them on notice that they were entitled to repayment of any medical bills they paid if the injured parties received a settlement from a third party. This became an issue that personal injury attorneys were forced to deal with in almost all personal injury cases with major medical bills.

The first thing we determine is whether there have been any double payments, meaning a medical bill has been paid by the automobile insurance company that does not have a right of reimbursement or subrogation. Second, we must determine the amount that was paid, and if any party has a right to be reimbursed for any portion of the payment. The law has developed over the last 20 years. You must consider whether the insurance is an HMO, PPO, or a self-funded ERISA plan; what language is contained in the plan, and whether it is a fully insured plan. When we receive notices that an insurance company is asserting its subrogation right, we immediately request copies of documents to review in order to determine whether the company does have that right. In some cases, the company may have the right to subrogation, but they may not, or it may be unclear and needs to be litigated in court.

If we determine that the insurance company does have a right of subrogation, we will attempt to negotiate a lower payment or request they pay a portion of our attorney's fees to keep more of the settlement money for our client. How successful we are in our negotiations largely depends on the circumstances. Sometimes there is limited insurance, and we do not want to work out a deal just to turn around and pay it all back to the insurance company. It really depends on the case, but it is very, very complicated. Medicare always has a right of subrogation, as do most worker's compensation carriers. Nevertheless, the steps are still the same: determine if they have a right, determine what bills they paid, and try to negotiate a lower amount to be paid back to the insurance carrier. There are many advantages of having an attorney involved in these situations because they are complicated and because attorneys can typically negotiate a lower payment than if the client tries to do this alone. Because the law has gotten progressively more complex regarding this issue, we spend more and more of our time each year dealing with who gets paid what and who gets reimbursed, all while trying to protect our client's interests first.

You may hear stories of people who get huge settlements and think that all of the money is paid to that person without ever realizing that there are many other parties who want their share of that money. I heard a story the other day about an attorney who did not tell his clients at the beginning of the case how much had to be paid back. It is so important to be up front with clients and explain that to them from the very beginning of the case. You try to negotiate a settlement with the insurance company that is in the best interest of your client, but you must be up front and warn the client in the beginning that this may be an issue in the case, because it is definitely something that people do not expect.

I had a situation with my own agent for the insurance company that covers my automobiles. She is a very competent agent and had written a policy for a friend, but did not factor in that if she selected the state's minimum coverage and an accident occurred, her health insurance would pay the bills but expect to be reimbursed from any settlement received from a third party. She really did not understand subrogation, and she is a competent insurance agent. At that point, she asked me to speak with the other agents to explain subrogation rights and to explain how the process works. Unfortunately, it is complicated and difficult to explain. The law concerning whether they must pay back a portion for attorney's fees and costs has been litigated for the past 20 years. The courts go back and forth in the case law on the subject because many of these plans are organized under federal law—more specifically, ERISA—and that is actually an issue for the United States Supreme Court. The decisions issued by the courts are difficult to understand. Some issues are yet to be resolved and are currently still being litigated in the court system. Therefore, you need a personal injury attorney who is dedicated to staying abreast of the latest developments and case laws in order to make sure that you receive the best possible settlement after determining what, if anything, must be paid back to insurance providers under subrogation rights. The best personal injury attorneys know the current laws, and are experienced in sifting through the complexities of subrogation rights to negotiate the best possible settlements for their clients.

PROTECT YOURSELF WITH THE RIGHT INSURANCE COVERAGE

Even though each state is different with regard to the minimum amount of insurance coverage required, we advise individuals to carry the maximum amount of coverage that they can afford, because if you are only carrying the state minimum requirements, in most cases, you are not really well protected in the event of an accident. Each individual really must determine what is best for them, but we feel that carrying more than the minimum state requirement is always better than opting for the state minimum coverage. For example, Pennsylvania requires that drivers have a minimum of $5,000 in medical coverage under their auto insurance policy; however, we suggest that you have at least $100,000 because of the subrogation issue. What most insurance agents fail to tell clients is that the difference in premium between $5,000 and $100,000 is not that much. It is actually very inexpensive to increase your coverage from the state minimum to $100,000. The insurance company does not disclose this because most auto accidents now exceed the $5,000 limit, so the insurance company is only required to pay $5,000 if the customer carries minimum state requirements.

Pennsylvania also has other types of insurance coverage that can protect motorists. For example, underinsured and uninsured coverage will protect you if you are injured in an accident by someone who only carries the state minimum insurance amounts. Agents either do not understand that, or do not explain it very well, because they typically sell a lower amount than the customer really needs, if they sell the coverage to them at all. Most customers come into an office and ask for the cheapest insurance policy available, but the insurance agent fails to explain to the customer that he could pay just a small amount more for exceptional coverage. My suggestion to readers would be to contact an attorney in your state that specializes in automobile accident cases or research some attorney websites for information about your state's insurance requirements, as well as optional insurance coverage you can purchase. In my experience, insurance agents do not necessarily sell customers the level of coverage they need to protect themselves because the agents do not really understand the claims process.

I will give you another example. This, of course, only applies in Pennsylvania because each state is a little different. However, in

Pennsylvania, if you are in an automobile accident and the other driver does not have insurance, you can make a claim under your uninsured motorist policy. Some states require that drivers carry uninsured coverage; however, Pennsylvania does not. We recommend that everyone purchase this additional coverage because in the event that you are in an accident and the other driver does not have insurance, you can go against your own insurance company for damages such as pain and suffering, lost income, and medical bills. Most of the time, if a driver does not have insurance, he also does not have any assets for you to pursue in a claim. Having uninsured coverage on your policy can compensate you for damages if the other driver has no insurance. Some states may have what we refer to as "no fault," as we do in Pennsylvania, so your own automobile insurance pays your medical bills. For readers who live in states that do not have "no fault," it works like this: Say that you have a child living with you, but she is injured while traveling in a vehicle with another person, and the accident is someone else's fault. Under Pennsylvania No Fault, your auto insurance will pay the medical bills up to your coverage amount. That is why it is so important to have extra coverage: it is inexpensive compared to the value you receive. That is also true for uninsured and underinsured coverage. Again, it is important that you determine what your state requires and purchase coverage to protect yourself based on that.

DOG BITE CASES

Switching gears again, I would like to discuss another type of personal injury case that I am familiar with: dog bites. I have been practicing law for over 31 years, and I have seen an increase in the number of dog bite cases in recent years. I do not mean to offend any pit bull owners; however, at least 50% of the dog bite cases I have seen involve pit bulls. It is very sad to see a young child with permanent facial disfigurement from a dog bite. One problem with pit bulls is that often the owners do not properly train the animals to curb their aggressive nature. The other issue is that once a pit bull bites, he causes more damage than other dogs because he does not release once he has bitten someone. It is unfortunate that we have seen an increase in these types of cases and that many of the cases involve children. In this type of personal injury case, a claim is made against the homeowner's or renter's insurance policy.

Some states have what is referred to as the "one bite rule," wherein you must prove that the dog has bitten a person before this incident in order to make a claim. That can be very difficult to do, as you may not be able to obtain that evidence. Pennsylvania repealed that rule. However, we still must prove that the dog had a vicious propensity, and that the owner knew, or should have known, that this dog might attack someone. If you can meet this burden of proof, you can then recover damages for medical bills, pain and suffering, and scarring. Sadly, in many cases, there is permanent scarring and nerve damage. Recently, I represented a young mother who was bitten so hard that she suffered nerve damage to her arm (she was trying to pull the dog off her son at the time of the bite).

A short time ago, I received information from the insurance industry that confirms dog bite cases have increased across the country. If you are injured due to a dog bite, you should contact a personal injury attorney immediately, because you must prove that the owner knew or should have known the dog was vicious. Because dog bite cases can be complex, having an experienced personal injury attorney will increase your chances of recovery, as they know how to handle any issues that come up in dog bite cases. Just because the dog bites someone does not mean you will definitely recover damages for your injury. That is why you need an experienced attorney who knows which doctors are competent, so that you can get the best treatment and recover with as little scarring as possible. Most attorneys treat dog bite cases as they do automobile cases and agree to a contingency fee arrangement, so there is no risk to the client. Furthermore, Pennsylvania requires that any settlement awarded to a minor must be approved by the court, and it may be required in many other states as well. This is another reason you need an attorney in these types of personal injury cases.

MOTORCYCLE ACCIDENT CASES

Another type of personal injury case my firm handles is motorcycle accidents. Most motorcycle accidents involve serious injury because there are no airbags to help protect the rider. In many cases, the accident is caused by another driver pulling out in front of a motorcycle, rather than the motorcycle driver speeding or driving recklessly, as many people may assume. Some people have the mentality that motorcycles are dangerous, so you must take this into consideration when you are determining the value of a case if you are headed into litigation. Motorcycle accident cases do have some differences; however, most attorneys who handle auto accident cases will also handle motorcycle accident cases. The issues regarding treatment of the injuries and knowing the best doctors to use are the same, even though there are some prejudices and other things that must be factored into these types of cases. For example, Pennsylvania does not require motorcyclists to carry medical coverage; therefore, you are almost always dealing with health insurance, and that brings you back to subrogation issues. We also have a cost containment provision in Pennsylvania that requires medical providers to reduce the cost of treatment to that which is approved by Medicare. Even with this in place, having an experienced personal injury attorney to deal with the medical providers and the insurance companies to negotiate the lowest payments possible results in more money for the client to compensate him or her for the pain and suffering, scarring, and other costs associated with the accident and/or injury.

In a way, this comes back to who you want to provide your medical treatment if you are injured in an accident. The advantage of having an experienced personal injury attorney is that he can recommend surgeons and doctors that he has worked with in the past and who he knows are well respected and proficient in their fields. After an accident, a client is usually treated at an emergency room or trauma center, and he may not know which doctor he should see for further treatment. On the other hand, symptoms may not present themselves immediately, and when they do, the client may not have the knowledge that a personal injury attorney has about spinal injuries, fractures, RSD, and other conditions associated with personal injury cases. I am not a doctor, but because of the experience I have reviewing doctors' testimony, reviewing medical records, and discussing various treatments and conditions with doctors, I have learned a good bit about medicine. I believe a good personal injury attorney must have a basic understanding of medicine to explain it to the insurance company, so they can understand what is involved concerning the proof of causation. Furthermore, if the case goes to trial, the attorney must be able to explain the injuries to the members of the jury in a way that they will understand.

Another issue that I deal with on a routine basis is the problem of doctors who do not want to cooperate, or do not want to spend their time testifying in a case. Since you cannot prove your case without medical testimony, we try to make it as convenient as possible for the doctors. If possible, we will videotape their testimony in their office and allow the other attorney to cross-examine the doctor at that time. However, if we must take the case to trial because the insurance company is refusing to agree to a fair settlement, I must know that I have a doctor who is willing to provide medical testimony to the jury, explaining that the injury is directly related to the accident, and discussing the treatment, future prognosis, and any limitations the client may have due to the injuries. Of course, the insurance company will present their own doctors to testify, and raise the issue that the injury is not really the result of the accident, or is not as severe as we claim. Therefore, I must know that I have a doctor who is on our side who will provide the best treatment possible for my client, who is willing to meet with me to discuss the injuries and treatment so that I understand them, and who will also be willing to provide testimony in court if necessary.

I have been practicing personal injury law for a very long time. I recall going to the medical center's library to research medical articles for information. Now I can find information online to help me understand certain medical conditions, look up a medical word that I am not familiar with, or learn about a treatment that I have not come across yet. Some doctors even have videotapes of the procedure to help you understand it, but most of the time I simply meet with the doctor so I can make sure I understand everything, and then review the report from the insurance company's doctor against what I have already learned from our own doctors and my own knowledge of that specific injury.

PREMISE LIABILITY CASES (ALSO KNOWN AS SLIP AND FALL ACCIDENTS)

The one thing that I want everyone to understand is that just because you fall on someone else's property, it does not necessarily mean you have a claim against that person. We receive calls about this and must explain that, to have a claim, you must prove fault. In order to prove fault, you must show that there was an unreasonably dangerous condition and that the landowner knew of the condition before your accident. Furthermore, because of comparative negligence, you must prove that you were not more than 50% at fault or, in other words, you were watching where you were going. If there were a hole in the ground that was covered, you had no way to know that the hole existed, you fell in and were hurt, then this is a pretty clear case of owner liability. Most cases, however, are not that clear.

There are also other elements, such as different standards based on who the property owner is, and what your relationship is with him or her. For example, if you are visiting a private home on a social visit, the standard of care is a little less than if you are on business property, because the business owner is inviting you onto his or her property to try to sell you something. Business owners have a higher standard of care to ensure that the property is safe for their customers, while, if you are on someone's private property just to visit them or you are there for your own business purposes, then the standard is not quite as high.

I once had a case in which a man went to work one morning, went through a door, washed up, walked out the same door, got into his truck, and was out working all day. After he left, someone dug a hole right outside the door but did not put any caution tape on the door or block it off. There was nothing to indicate that there was a hole outside this door. My client returned at the end of the day, entered through another door, washed up, and walked out of the door he used that morning. Since it was nighttime, he could not see. He fell into the hole, injured his spine, and had to have two spinal surgeries. In that case, I thought that the liability was pretty clear, but the insurance company did not agree and made us litigate the case (they ultimately conceded on day two of the trial).

To me, the liability was so clear because he had no way of knowing the hole was there, and the company did nothing to prevent someone from walking out of that door such as using caution tape or covering the hole. On the other end of the spectrum, imagine that you are in a grocery store, and you slip and fall because another customer spills some of her water. The water was only there for a few seconds, and the store did not have any way of knowing the other customer would spill her water. That would be a very tough case in which to prove liability. However, if a store employee was mopping the floor, did not put up any warning signs, and you fell; that would be a clearer case of liability.

I can give you many examples of cases we have handled over the years, but there is another category within premises liability where we have seen an increase in volume, and that is 'falling on ice' cases. In Pennsylvania, as in some other states, we have a doctrine that we refer to as the Hills and Ridges Doctrine. The courts have ruled that if you slip and fall on black or clear ice or fresh snow, you cannot recover. However, if the surface has hills and ridges, such as snow that has been piled up for days and is not smooth because people have been walking across it, then you can recover damages from slipping and falling. The basis for the law is that in the northern states that receive more snow and ice, property owners cannot continuously be outside clearing their property of ice and snow. Therefore, the snow or ice must have been there for some time in order for you to recover from a slip and fall. There are some local ordinances in certain municipalities that require landowners to clear ice within a certain period of time. Unfortunately, the Hills and Ridges Doctrine has developed in a way that has allowed courts to throw out cases if the client even mentions he slipped on smooth ice.

That is another reason to talk to an attorney right away. Not because we are going to tell you to lie, but we are going to remind you about the law. When people fall, they are often embarrassed and, usually, the last thing they are thinking about is a personal injury claim. Insurance companies will try to get statements to use against you later, which is why you need a personal injury attorney to advise you of your rights before you give any statements about the accident. A personal injury attorney can sort out the facts to advise you if you have a case, then develop that case to recover damages to compensate you for your injuries, medical bills, and lost wages.

TRUCK ACCIDENTS

In my experience, very few truck drivers will ever admit fault because to do so is to jeopardize their livelihoods. Truck drivers are also required to carry extensive insurance because they are more prone to being involved in a very serious accident than regular drivers are. Typically, the insurance company has a law firm on retainer, so that as soon as an accident occurs, the attorneys and investigators immediately begin work to determine what happened. Most truck accident cases cause serious injuries due to the size of the truck. If you or a loved one has been injured, or if a loved one has been killed in a truck accident, you should contact an attorney as soon as possible to protect yourself and your family. You want an attorney working for you immediately to gather data from the accident scene and the truck's recorder box before evidence is degraded or the information is erased.

For example, about six months ago a woman I knew lost her husband in a truck accident. I immediately contacted the trucking company, and I forwarded it what is called a "spoliation letter." This letter contains a list of approximately 30 to 40 items that we want to preserve, such as the data recorder, truck logs, and maintenance records. It is critical that you have that before items are changed, lost, or do not exist anymore. In these types of cases, you need a personal injury attorney as soon as possible so that he can deal with the truck company on your behalf. You want a personal injury attorney who has experience in truck accident cases and knows which qualified liability experts and mechanical experts to contact. You need to get the evidence as quickly as possible and stay in front of the case. The accident happened on Saturday; I found out about it on Sunday, and by Monday, I had determined who owned the truck and sent the letter to them. Even though I acted that quickly and informed the company not to destroy information, they drove the truck and erased information. However, because I sent the letter, my client was protected. Because the letter was sent, if the owner tries to deny information, the jury will at least receive a charge, and that will create a presumption that the evidence that was destroyed was against the trucking company. In these cases, we want to preserve the data, but we also need qualified people who can download the information. We have people whom we can call who know the technology used and can go out right away to obtain the information we need.

The best advice I can give to anyone injured in a truck accident is that it is better to have a personal injury attorney on your side sooner than later. You need someone who knows what is required of truck drivers and has the resources to get the right people in the right place as soon as possible to gather information and preserve evidence. Trucking companies and their insurance companies have unlimited resources, and they will always spend whatever is necessary to defend these cases; therefore, contacting a personal injury attorney with experience in truck accident cases as quickly as possible is imperative.

DRUNK DRIVING ACCIDENTS

Just like trucking accident cases and motorcycle accident cases, drunk driving cases are a separate category of personal injury cases. When I have a drunk driver on the other side of a case, I know that I can claim punitive damages in addition to compensatory damages. Compensatory damages are intended to make the person "whole" again. Juries determine what amount of money should be paid to the injured party to compensate him for their pain and suffering, medical bills, the loss of income, how the injured party's quality of life has changed due to the accident, and how the accident has affected his family and its activities. We explain compensatory damages to the jury in terms of what amount of money will make the person "whole," or in other words, compensate them for what has been taken away from them. However, in contrast, the purpose of punitive damages is to punish the person for their behavior and deter him or her from repeating that behavior. In the case of a drunk driver, punitive damages are meant to send a message to the driver to deter him from driving while intoxicated again.

For example, in an accident case in which the person was speeding, the insurance company may admit that the driver was at fault, and then it is just a matter of how much the jury will compensate this person. There is no discussion about how fast the person was driving or how reckless he may have been driving when the accident occurred. However, in a drunk driving case, even if the insurance company admits fault, you can still bring in the fact that the driver was intoxicated at the time the accident occurred because you have the separate issue of the punitive damages claim. Also, juries hear this testimony and they tend to factor that into the amount of compensatory damages they award, as well as the amount of punitive damages for the drunk driving. It can benefit the injured party because insurance companies are not required to pay punitive damage awards; however, if the jury awards more in compensatory damages because they do not "like" the drunk driver, it means more money for the injured party. In addition, if the jury awards a large personal verdict against the defendant and the insurance company could have settled the case, the insurance company could face a bad faith claim. These are some of the aspects of drunk driving cases that are different from other automobile accident cases. Having a personal injury attorney with experience in drunk driving cases benefits the injured party, because the attorney can factor in all of these elements and determine the value of the claim when considering how much a jury might pay based on the evidence at hand, and the elements of the damages claimed by the plaintiff.

SOCIAL MEDIA AND PERSONAL INJURY CASES

Social media has become an element of personal injury cases, because attorneys never know what a client may post on social media sites. The courts in Pennsylvania are still trying to determine what defense attorneys are entitled to access with regard to social media sites. Some defense attorneys have petitioned the court for access to the social media websites of plaintiffs by requesting the plaintiff's passwords. There have been some cases in which an attorney or his staff have "friended" the plaintiff so they could gain access to the plaintiff's social media sites. Of course, this is not permitted, and the plaintiff's attorney will object because neither the defense attorney nor anyone employed by him is permitted to contact the plaintiff directly. All communication between the parties must be through their respective attorneys.

There was another case in which the attorney advised his client to alter or erase information that the client had on his Facebook page and then to lie under oath about the information during a deposition. That was completely unethical, and I am sure the attorney was certainly disciplined for his behavior. That is just another issue with social media: once the information is there, you are not permitted to change it then claim it was never there.

You must be very careful what you post to social media during a personal injury case. For example, if you are claiming a back injury, but you are posting on social media that you were out dancing the night away, that is going to hurt your case. First of all, you should not be out dancing when you are claiming a back injury, but you most certainly should not be boasting of it by posting messages on Facebook. This is the type of thing that defense attorneys claim they are entitled to access. So far, I have objected to their motions, claiming they are not entitled to anything on social media. Even though they may be entitled to something, what they are entitled to has not been settled in the courts. I would say to anyone, not just those involved in personal injury cases, that you must be very careful about what you post on social media because you do not know who will have access to that information and how it could hurt you in years to come. Once it is there, it is there forever. Yes, it is an issue for attorneys in the practice of personal injury, but it is also an issue for anyone trying to decide what information to post on social media and how much they should use social media.

In summary, if you have a personal injury claim, you should talk to an experienced personal injury attorney. If you do not know a personal injury attorney, ask friends or family who may have been through a personal injury case for their recommendations. You want to make sure that you retain a firm that limits its practice to personal injury cases and that you will be dealing primarily with an attorney that has experience, not his associate or his paralegal. You should also hire an attorney who is willing to take the case on a contingency fee basis. It is in your best interest to take advantage of the free initial consultation to find out what your options are and if you have a claim. It is also to your benefit to do this sooner rather than later because with each passing day, things could be happening that could have an adverse affect on your case. Once these things occur, there may be nothing the attorney can do to mitigate the damage. My best advice: if you have a personal injury claim, talk to an experienced personal injury attorney as soon as possible following the accident.

(This content should be used for informational purposes only. It does not create an attorney-client relationship with any reader and should not be construed as legal advice. If you need legal advice, please contact an attorney in your community who can assess the specifics of your situation.)

8

WHY YOU SHOULD HIRE A PERSONAL INJURY ATTORNEY

by Mark R. Gaertner Esq.

Mark R. Gaertner Esq.
Walsh & Gaertner, PA
Saint Paul, Minnesota

Mark Gaertner is a personal injury and wrongful death lawyer who represents individuals and families who have been injured as a result of an accident. He has served as a lawyer in a number of cases that led to notable settlements. Mark is a former insurance defense lawyer. The insurance defense background allows him to make an accurate assessment of the case and anticipate the strategies of the insurance companies. Mark has been recognized as a Minnesota Super Lawyer by his peers. He is licensed to practice law in Minnesota and Wisconsin and is a Minnesota Supreme Court Qualified Neutral.

As a personal injury and wrongful death lawyer, he has represented thousands of individuals and families who have suffered death or injury as a result of an accident. Having been an insurance defense attorney, he understands how insurance companies evaluate the potential success of a claim, and can present the merits of a case in a way that will lead to the highest possible award for his clients. As a successful trial lawyer, if the insurance company is not willing to provide a fair settlement, he is prepared to go to trial to get what's just for his clients.

WHY YOU SHOULD HIRE A PERSONAL INJURY ATTORNEY

There are several reasons why you should hire a personal injury attorney after being injured in an accident. The first has to do with peace of mind. Dealing with insurance companies, their adjusters, and their attorneys can be a headache for anyone; it can be especially challenging for someone who has just been injured in an automobile accident. While the attorney is dealing with the insurance company, you can take care of yourself and concentrate fully on getting the medical treatment necessary to recover from your injuries. You gain all of the benefits by hiring a personal injury attorney without incurring any of the up-front costs. Most personal injury attorneys work on a contingency fee basis, which means that you have the benefit of having an attorney represent your interests without paying him, until, and unless, he obtains a settlement for you.

To me, it is just good, old-fashioned common sense to hire a personal injury attorney. You will not be paying the attorney out of your pocket, but he is doing all of this work for you and protecting your rights. You will already have enough to worry about trying to figure out a way to pay your medical bills, get to and from doctor's appointments, pay for medical treatments and medicine; all while trying to figure out possible claims, who may be sued, and the timing of a settlement. Rather than taking on all of that, you can hire an attorney to deal with the paperwork and the people while you take care of the most important thing: getting better. Your life is already busy without dealing with litigation. There is no room left on your plate for dealing with insurance companies and adjusters. Therefore, it is valuable to have someone as your advocate who is not going to charge you anything unless he wins a settlement for you. Even if I were not a personal injury attorney, this no-risk scenario offering great benefits would be a "no-brainer" for me.

Another advantage of hiring a personal injury attorney has to do with the settlement. Having an attorney negotiate with the insurance company typically results in a larger settlement amount than if you attempt to handle the case on your own. One of the ways an attorney does this is through experience and knowledge of the process. Since personal injury attorneys deal with insurance companies on a daily basis, they know what to expect from these companies. Some insurance companies may try to hide facts or portray the case in a more favorable light for themselves. However, it is essential to have an experienced personal injury attorney to separate the bad insurance information from the good insurance information if you want to obtain a fair and just settlement. For example, an insurance company may offer a settlement, but buried within the fine print of the settlement forms is a clause waiving your right to other claims of which you are not currently aware. It is important to keep in mind that insurance adjusters are trying to save the company money and are not there to advise you of all of your rights. A personal injury attorney will protect you from settling a claim that is not in your best interest.

In my experience, some insurance companies will tell clients that they are receiving all of the money allowed under the policy. The clients agree, thinking they are receiving everything to which they are entitled for their injuries without realizing there may be more legitimate claims to be made in the future. Hiring a personal injury attorney means that you are protected from these types of settlement releases, because your attorney will make sure that all of your potential future claims are protected before advising you to agree to sign any release.

Calculating the value of a case is another reason to hire an experienced personal injury attorney. Most often, this is the most difficult part of a personal injury case. Clients may have read internet articles or news items leading them to assume their case is worth as much as another case with similar factors. For example, a client may have read that someone with two broken legs received a $2 million settlement and assume that his personal injury case is also worth $2 million. Much information may be left out of the story, such as the fact that the judge actually lowered the jury-awarded $2 million figure to $10,000 because the case did not warrant such large damages.

The one thing that influences people's idea of the value of their case is media coverage of large-scale cases. Either people believe their case should be worth as much as the amount received by someone for spilling drive-through hot coffee on themselves, or that their case will not be worth as much because they are too young or old. Some of the elderly believe that their case is worth very little because they already have aches and pains. On the contrary, it takes the knowledge and experience of a personal injury attorney to determine the true value of a case; one who has worked with countless in-state and out-of-state insurance companies and who has participated in and watched case after case being settled, and tried by juries.

Each personal injury case is different. Unless you have day-to-day knowledge and experience in valuing a case, you may be reaching too high or selling yourself out too low. For example, some people assume that their case is not worth much money because they only missed two days of work and had one trip to the emergency room. In reality, they may have other claims that should be addressed before settlement. Insurance companies want to pay the lowest figure possible while personal injury attorneys want to ensure that their clients receive a fair and just settlement for their injuries.

IF YOU'RE NOT REPRESENTED BY A PERSONAL INJURY ATTORNEY

What people often do not understand is that insurance companies have special adjusters to handle claims in which the injured person is not represented by an attorney. These adjusters are masters of manipulation. They will befriend the claimant, even telling them that they do not really need a lawyer and that they can handle the claim themselves. The adjuster will call "just to check" on the individual to see how he or she is feeling. Eventually, after the person feels comfortable trusting the adjuster, he will tell the claimant that he has reviewed the case and the most his case is worth is $1,000, and that may be pushing the limit. The adjuster will work hard to convince the claimant that he only wants what is in the claimant's best interest and, just because he feels for the claimant, he is going to bat for him and get him the full $1,000. Since the claimant feels he can trust this adjuster as a nice person who cares about him, the claimant accepts the settlement and signs the release forms. Unfortunately, by the time the injured claimant comes to our office because he is experiencing more pain or other health issues related to the accident, there is usually nothing we can do because he has signed a full claims release, even though he swears the adjuster said he could get more money if the injury got worse.

Experienced personal injury attorneys know the court system, are familiar with insurance companies, and know which ones pay more than others do. They know the types of claims that will garner higher jury verdicts or evoke a sympathetic response. Good personal injury attorneys keep up with the latest jury verdicts and insurance settlements so they know exactly what is being received by their firm as well as other law firms. The young claimant who feels his claim is not worth much because of his age, needs a personal injury attorney to explain to him that his claim may be worth a great deal, as the injury could affect his life and his ability to obtain certain jobs. Elderly people often need to understand that they are living in their golden years and have the right to enjoy this time free from the pain caused by another's negligence, even if they are already dealing with existing pain. Personal injury attorneys help individuals by protecting their rights and seeing that they receive a fair and just settlement for their claims, regardless of their age at the time of the injury.

Another benefit of hiring a personal injury attorney is having someone that can manage your case from the very beginning all the way through settlement or a trial. A new client is typically concerned about the results of the damage to their vehicle: whose insurance company will repair or replace their vehicle, how they are going to pay their deductible, and if they are going to be provided with a rental car. Most clients assume that a personal injury attorney only helps them with their physical injuries. However, I believe that a personal injury attorney should help his clients with all facets of the case, from helping them work through the process of dealing with the insurance company to settling the property damage claim once the final damages have been determined. Even clients with serious physical injuries will still be concerned with transportation to work, or to the doctor; and who is going to pay for that. Dealing with the paperwork can be overwhelmingly stressful for our clients, which is why we jump in at the very beginning to help our clients take care of their immediate needs so that we can move on to more important case elements. It is easy for clients to focus on their immediate needs to the point that they even forget their severe injuries. By helping our clients take care of those immediate needs we help them move forward onto the next phase of the personal injury case.

A personal injury attorney's help can be invaluable; from filing the necessary paperwork (property damage claim settlements, and medical bill payments) to proper representation when the claimant is giving a recorded statement. Insurance companies love for claimants to give recorded statements without their attorney present, so that anything that is said during that interview can be used against the claimant later in the case. I do not believe that it hurts a client to give a statement to the insurance company if the client's attorney is present during the interview.

WHAT IF AN INSURANCE COMPANY RED FLAGS YOUR CASE

Another aspect of the personal injury settlement process is to deal with the insurance companies' investigators who deal with certain "red flags" that show up in a personal injury case. These investigators are part of what is known as the Special Investigations Unit, or SIU. For a post-injury example, if my client continues to be treated by a chiropractor that he has seen for his entire life but the chiropractor charges more for each treatment than other providers, the insurance company may flag this and send it to a special investigative unit. That red flag will make the future more difficult for the client and the attorney.

Another example would be; if you were involved in an automobile accident in a specific area of town or a specific intersection, your case may be red-flagged by the insurance company and sent to special investigations. Since attorneys know this, we can begin to prepare for a much more difficult case as we go through each process. While no one at the insurance company would admit this, a client's ethnicity is going to have an effect on his or her claim, whether the client is from Somalia or Laos and goes to a particular doctor, or is a carpenter by profession. Therefore, we begin preparing for that from the beginning of the case. Another red flag could be as simple as an entire family being injured in the same car and all family members being treated by the same physician. While it makes sense that a family would all visit the same doctor, it could cause the insurance company to make negotiating a settlement more difficult. Even though this sounds illogical, we need to prepare them for the situation if it comes up.

When attorneys begin evaluating a case, we look for areas that may cause a red flag: location, ethnicity of the client, and the medical providers being used for treatment. We immediately begin to prepare for these issues by getting ready for the insurance company to request a formal statement or our client's deposition. The insurance company is going to want to put our client under oath, dig into the claim, and do whatever is necessary to avoid paying the claim. If the claim fits into one of these "red flag" areas, we know that we will have a much more difficult fight on our hands, because the areas and budgets change yearly for these special SIU divisions.

On the other hand, I will say this about the SIU process. Insurance companies are attempting to put the "bad guys" out of business and there are many of these deceitful individuals in Minnesota due to its status as a "no-fault" state. Since a great deal of money has been paid in relation to no-fault claims in Minnesota, numerous out-of-state providers have set up toll-free numbers and opened their own clinics to treat injured victims. They abuse the system for a few years and then they disappear. These types of providers are not interested in the well-being or the health of their clients. They are simply interested in getting as much money from the insurance company as possible for a claim. Many insurance companies have worked hard to put them out of business, and stop the fraud and abuse of Minnesota's no-fault system. If we have clients come to us who are being treated in one of these clinics, we immediately notify them of the situation and then prepare for the "red flag" that will ultimately be attached to their claim as we move through the settlement process. Unfortunately, many people are fooled into believing these providers are looking out for their interests because they are innocent to the system's abuses. Most clients decide on their own to switch clinics.

This is why I truly believe that clients must be prepared from the very beginning of the process and be kept informed as we take each step toward settling or litigating their claim. Even when a client has a "red flag" issue, an experienced attorney knows how to weed through the issues and avoid the pitfalls so that they can achieve a successful outcome for the client. Some attorneys find this process too difficult, preferring to prepare the case for immediate litigation and a trial to avoid the tough work associated with trying to negotiate a settlement of the case.

COMMON SENSE CAN LEAD TO THE BEST SETTLEMENT

However, I believe it is very important to always have an eye towards settlement, even when your case is in the litigation phase. I try to position each of my cases in such a way that the other side wants to settle. Filing the right motions, serving the right discovery, and creatively using common sense helps bring forth the best possible settlement for my clients. Some attorneys with an "either/or" mentality get fixated on either trying the case or settling the case, but they never consider these solutions to be interchangeable. Having previously worked in the defense industry, I know that insurance companies are always interested in settlement if they are given a compelling reason to do so. Sometimes that may mean filing a motion for punitive damages or taking the depositions of the right people. If I make the insurance company nervous by bringing in other parties and serving discovery, they will find it difficult to answer without admitting to something they would rather keep quiet, it increases my settlement possibilities and makes my trial easier.

Personally, I think of it as a "common sense" approach to practicing law. Law school students are taught to focus on case law, which may cause some attorneys to lose sight of the common sense element of practicing law. For example, when you have multiple parties in a lawsuit, such as two or three defendants, sometimes aligning yourself with one party may be what you need to make your case stronger. Evaluating each case individually and deciding how to get the other side to want to pay money, has been lost as attorneys want to brag about how many cases they have tried. In my mind, that is a failure on the part of an attorney to be unable to settle disputes without the intervention of the court. My colleagues may scoff at that statement, but I believe that from the moment my client enters my office it is my job to help the client recover from his injuries and to get him the best possible settlement.

SEEING THE RIGHT MEDICAL PROVIDERS

A distinct advantage of hiring a personal injury attorney is having someone to manage the entire process from the beginning of the case through to the end. Most of our clients come to us after they have already seen at least one, if not more than one, medical provider. Due to our experience in the personal injury field, we have compiled two lists of medical providers (doctors, neurologists, chiropractors, etc.) who have worked with previous clients and who have reported either good or bad results.

The first order of business with a new client is to compare his current list of medical providers with both of our lists to advise the client if he is being treated by a doctor on one of those lists or a doctor with whom we have never dealt. If the doctor is not on either list, we will want the client's permission to communicate with the doctor. That way, we can make sure that the doctor is not one of those "red-flag" doctors, and get feedback from our client about his medical care so that we can add this doctor to the appropriate list. While we do not interfere with the doctor or his treatment plan, in our experience we have learned that some doctors will get in the way of either a settlement or favorable award by refusing to participate in the litigation process or failing to provide the best medical treatment.

To stay on the same page with the doctor, we will routinely order copies of the client's medical records for progress updates for our files and in order to discuss his medical treatment progress with the client. There have been times when our client reports that he must have surgery but when we refer to the medical records, the physician has not referred to a required surgery. This can be due to a misunderstanding on the part of our client, an incorrect medical transcription, or the physician's forgetfulness in mentioning the surgery in the paperwork.

Since this can have a significant impact on the case, as attorneys, we must remain vigilant about reviewing medical records. Whatever the reason might be for the mistake, the mistake must be corrected before trial. Therefore, we monitor the medical records and the treatment providers throughout the entire case. We will meet with doctors, have telephone conferences, and visit their offices. Staying in contact with the client and his medical providers ensures that we are all on the same page and that we are working for the benefit of our client.

LANDMINES THAT CAN HURT YOUR CASE

As personal injury attorneys, we weave through the landmines and the red flags while getting the medical bills paid, and our clients move toward maximum recovery and a settlement—unless the case needs to go to trial. Part of the case process includes preparing our clients in the event that we do not settle. Courtrooms make some people nervous and uncomfortable, even those that may think they want their day in court. We explain the process to them and even practice answering questions in a "mock trial" setting to help them feel more comfortable and at ease. Even then, taking a year to prepare someone for a court appointment won't eliminate the possibility that he may "freeze up" in the courtroom. If the case does not go well and the jury does not respond to him, the client may end up with nothing. Some clients are better at speaking in public than others and having the right attorney may help. However, when it comes down to it, if the client is not able to be convincing in court, there may be a problem. The best you can do is practice, prepare, and do your job to the best of your ability.

On another note, I would like to discuss medical bills and insurance companies. In Minnesota, if your no-fault coverage pays your medical bills, you are not required to pay those funds back to your no-fault provider, though there are a few exceptions. For example, commercial vehicle involvement or out-of-state accidents may result in requirements to repay the no-fault insurer for the incurred cost of medical bills. Real issues crop up in cases where people have reached the $20,000 cap of their no-fault insurance policy. At that point, the medical insurance company or Medicare may start paying the medical bills associated with the automobile accident. In most cases, you are required to reimburse your health insurance company or Medicare from any settlement funds that you receive from the at-fault party's insurance company.

It is important to review the language contained in the health insurance policy to determine the extent of its subrogation rights (the right to be reimbursed). Some policies contain language that grants the insurance company subrogation rights in all cases. However, there are some policies stating that the company is only entitled to receive funds in a settlement after the injured person has been paid everything to which he is entitled, with funds remaining to pay the health insurance provider. Our negotiation with the health insurance provider will depend on the policy's contents. I believe it is important to tackle this issue early on by getting a copy of the policy and knowing in advance the provisions for subrogation rights. Early negotiations with the health insurance provider prior to receiving any settlement funds can improve your position, rather than waiting until after you receive a settlement. You may be able to come to an agreement for a 50% repayment to the health insurance provider if you receive a beneficial settlement for your client.

Settling Medicare subrogation rights is a bit different. Since Medicare has constantly changing rules, you basically submit the settlement amount and attorney's fees and costs to Medicare, and then Medicare will come back with the owed figure. However, I advise attorneys to require a copy of the Medicare report, detailing exactly what was paid on behalf of the client. Many times when you review the detailed list of payments, you will find Medicare payments that were not associated with injuries sustained in the accident; those payments should not be reimbursed. Many people miss this step of filing an appeal with Medicare to request that these charges be removed, so a new figure can be calculated. This is a way to put more money in your client's pocket. Medical assistance is another way to put money in people's pockets when people do not have car insurance and medical assistance pays the bills. Medical assistance also has the right to be paid back, but there is room to negotiate those claims.

One case in particular comes to my mind because it was so tragic, and there appeared to be nothing that could be done to help the family with the staggering medical bills. While on summer break, three young relatives were on their way to go fishing when the driver fell asleep. My client, who was sitting in the back seat, was ejected and suffered severe, life-threatening injuries. All three families of the young men were devastated. My client was in the ICU for a couple of months. The medical bills far exceeded the $20,000 available in medical coverage. By the time my client's family came to me, they had already consulted two other attorneys and were advised that there was nothing more to do. My client's family did not want to sue their family members but they did not know what to do about the massive medical bills they were facing. We found four different insurance policies on this particular case that paid medical bills and provided money for future medical treatments, the purchase of a special van, and modifications to the home that included a special handicap ramp. This would have never been possible if we did not find these insurance policies so that no one had to pay any money out of their own pockets other than the insurance companies. It has been five years and the family still stays in contact with us to provide updates. Once, they invited us over for dinner and it was really satisfying to see that we were able to make a difference in their lives. At the time we entered the case, our clients felt that the only way to pay for medical bills and necessary home modifications was by suing their family members, which would have devastated the entire family. We were able to settle with the various insurance companies, make sure bills were paid, and ensure that the young survivor's needs were provided for, without the other family members paying a dime.

PEDESTRIANS INJURED IN AN ACCIDENT

Switching gears a little bit, I would like to talk about pedestrian cases. We have people that contact our office when a child has been struck by a vehicle and they do not believe they have a case because it was a child that was injured. Nearly every police report that I have ever read states that "The child darted out." I think "dart" is a word that police officers are taught when they are learning how to write a police report. Therefore, if a child is injured, the police report will state that the child darted out and the insurance company is going to deny responsibility. People have been led to believe they do not have a case in these instances. We have handled many, many pedestrian cases where we were able to overturn that "darted out" comment. For example, when we depose the police officer we ask him if he was on the scene when it happened. Of course, he replies that he was not. We then ask him who said that the child darted out and the officer will reply that the driver told him this when he arrived on the scene. We also ask if the driver actually said "darted out" because that is not a typical phrase used in everyday language. When we depose the driver, we ask him what happened and he will usually state that he never saw the child. Therefore, how could he have seen the child "dart out" when he never saw the child? Right there, we have just won the case by taking the time to properly investigate the case from the very beginning. We talk to the police officer and the driver, and we search for witnesses to depose. We search to find a neighbor that may have been working in her front yard or looking out of his window at the time of the accident. The biggest hurdle in these cases is convincing the insurance company that the child did not dart out.

In one case, a 78-year old woman was crossing the street and the police report said she darted out in front of the bus. I do not know many 78-year old women that can dart out in front of a bus. The insurance company denied the claim even though it was clear that the driver never saw the woman. Through investigation and interviews, we are often able to convince the insurance company that the driver was at fault and the person, whether a child or a 78-year old woman, did not "dart out" as the police report may have stated. Unfortunately, people take the word of the insurance company when they are told that the accident is really their fault, rather than consulting an experienced personal injury attorney. I cannot stress enough that through proper investigation and a lot of paperwork, the rewards for the client can be great. The client may feel hopeless, and that they will never receive compensation for their injuries and medical bills, because of the police report. However, in most cases, there are witnesses in the neighborhood that the police may never have interviewed, so it is critically important to conduct a proper investigation.

In some cases, it's necessary to conduct several interviews of the client, the driver, and any witnesses because the stories do not make any sense. From where the witness was standing, it might be impossible to see the client based on what the driver said. Sometimes statements do not match up when reviewed against the evidence at the accident scene. If the victim was transported to the hospital, the police officer may have not taken the victim's statement. Most times, the police officer was not present at the scene of the accident, so all of the information he received for his report comes from the driver's point of view. In order to win these types of cases, the attorney must dig in and do his own investigation to discover information that will convince an insurance company or a jury that his client was not at fault and deserves a fair and just settlement for his injuries.

SOCIAL MEDIA CAN ONLY HURT YOUR CASE

One very important issue, regarding the reason why people need to consult an attorney if they are involved in an automobile accident, comes down to information transfer. A person involved in an accident will post something on Facebook, tell their friends and relatives the story, and discuss the details of the accident with the insurance adjuster. They are relying on this information to determine if they have a case. However, unless their family and friends are experienced personal injury attorneys, their advice is not always accurate. The insurance adjuster does not want you to consult with an attorney because it is the adjuster's job to pay as little as possible to settle this claim. Therefore, the injured party is making a decision based on inaccurate and biased information. However, most personal injury attorneys offer a free consultation where you can sit down and discuss your case with an experienced attorney. I also believe that you should talk with the attorney and not a paralegal or legal secretary. The attorney will go through the facts of the case with you and advise you if you do in fact have a case to pursue. Typically, if you do want to pursue the case it will cost you nothing up front, as the attorney will accept the case on a contingency basis so that he only is paid if you receive money.

Social media also impacts personal injury cases in another way. People post comments to social media about their accident, others reply, and the conversation continues. Insurance companies will use what is said on social media against you at trial. You should never post comments about your accident to social media because the insurance companies will be watching. For example, your friend may say, "You are such a faker" when you post a comment about injuring your back and neck. The insurance company will bring this up as well as your comment back that said, "LOL, I am just trying to get money from the insurance company." While all of this was innocent fun, it just damaged your personal injury claim. My office monitors what our clients post to social media, and sends constant reminders advising them not to talk about their case on social media. While you may be the most honest person in the world, things that you post can still be taken out of context and misinterpreted. One intentionally funny comment can be turned into a damaging comment by the insurance company at trial.

Photographs are another problem with social media. For instance, if you state during your deposition that you cannot play golf due to your back injury, but then post a picture of yourself on the 18th green on Facebook, we have a problem. There you are, telling the world the great sunny weather conditions where you just played the best round of golf in your life, while claiming that you cannot work due to a back injury. Insurance companies have ways of discovering these things. What clients must remember is that things that are supposed to be private still have a way of finding their way into the open in today's media-saturated world.

I see more cases of social media hurting a case than ever helping a case. My advice to clients is to never make any reference to the accident, the case, or the progress of the case on social media sites. Clients should not talk about the fact that they had to give a deposition today, or they hate the idea of testifying at trial. Keep in mind that anything you say can potentially be used against you; the defendants, insurance companies, and their attorneys have ways of finding what you post. The insurance company can file motions for your passwords to access your social media sites to see what you are posting. Before posting anything, think about how this might look if it was to come up in a deposition or at trial. If in doubt, you should ask your attorney before posting the comment or, better yet, do not post it at all.

(This content should be used for informational purposes only. It does not create an attorney-client relationship with any reader and should not be construed as legal advice. If you need legal advice, please contact an attorney in your community who can assess the specifics of your situation.)

9

THE MANY AREAS A PERSONAL INJURY ATTORNEY WILL HELP YOU

by Christian Anouge II, Esq.

Christian Anouge II, Esq.
The Anouge Law Firm
Ocoee, Florida

Christian Anouge II, Esq. is a founding member of the Anouge Law Firm, and a leading Personal Injury/Wrongful Death attorney in Central Florida. Chris began his career on the "other side" defending insurance companies, but ultimately found his passion in fighting for the individual instead. Compassionate empathy for "the little guy" combined with his twenty years of experience in negotiating, litigating, and aggressively advocating for thousands of clients has honed Chris' keen ability to analyze a case from all angles. Chris' savvy for the nuances in the law, along with personalized attention to detail combine to produce the best strategy for each client on a case by case basis.

THE MANY AREAS A PERSONAL INJURY ATTORNEY WILL HELP YOU

There are many reasons why you should hire a personal injury attorney. First, a personal injury attorney will help you to evaluate your claim. Typically, most individuals who are involved in an automobile accident are dealing with this process for the first time, so they don't know the value of their claims or how to calculate such a figure. However, personal injury attorneys often deal with multiple automobile accident cases, which makes them better equipped to determine the value of your case. Personal injury attorneys subscribe to services such as "jury verdict reporters," which provide details of jury verdicts for similar cases in your jurisdiction, enabling the attorney to provide an informed opinion on the range of values for your particular case.

Another way that a personal injury attorney helps victims is by making sure they seek proper medical treatment for injuries. After an accident, it could take a couple of days or even longer to feel the pain from sustained injuries. Immediately after the accident, shock sets in, and then concern about your intended destination when the accident occurred (or what's needed for repairs and transportation), so that injuries usually end up taking a "back seat" on your priority list. An attorney can help you determine the next step by slowing down the process and help you evaluate your claim. For example, you may have a stiff neck immediately following the accident; but a month later, you may discover after an MRI that you actually have a herniated disc. An attorney can help make sure that you receive the proper tests and treatments after an accident so that injuries don't go undiagnosed.

Attorneys can also help you navigate the legal system, offering advice on necessary deadlines so that you are not barred from bringing an action in court or filing a claim against your insurance company. They will help you negotiate medical bills to keep more money in your pocket. Attorneys will advise you on sources of insurance or funds that can help pay for your medical bills. In Florida, for instance, personal injury protection is a type of medical payment coverage tied in to automobile insurance policies.

There is one overwhelmingly important reason to hire an experienced personal injury attorney: paperwork. Your attorney will review and explain the paperwork requested by the insurance company before you agree to sign the forms. Some insurance companies may try to get you to sign an early release. Hiring (or at least consulting with) an attorney before signing any release form can be important; some of these releases contain waivers of future claims. By signing a waiver, you may not be entitled to file a claim in the future if you discover an undiagnosed injury at a later date.

Some insurance companies in Florida are notorious for sending an adjuster to the accident scene in one of their rapid response vehicles. The adjuster will talk to you at the accident scene, ask a few questions, and may even say that you do not need an attorney. They will tell you that they can "settle your claim right now" so that you can quickly have money in your pocket, but you will need to sign a release. Without carefully reading the release, you may assume that the offered money is for vehicle repairs; however, the release may actually be waiving your right to bring a future claim for injuries. Even though the insurance adjuster may not clearly explain this, it is very difficult to have the releases set aside later if you realize that you have suffered untreated injuries from the accident.

An attorney helps protect you against insurance adjusters who try to settle too quickly. Depending on the type of injury, it may be necessary to see a chiropractor, an orthopedic doctor, or another medical specialist. You are not limited to seeing your family doctor after an accident. An attorney will help direct you to the types of specialists that should be seen, depending on the severity of your injuries. Furthermore, your attorney will advise you that under Florida Personal Injury Protection (PIP) law, you have the right to see any physician you choose, and the PIP coverage will pay monies towards that physician's bill up to a certain limit. (The limits vary by state and depend on whether that state requires PIP to be carried on an insurance policy.) These are just some of the reasons why you should consult with an attorney when you are injured in an accident. An attorney will advise you of your rights so that you can make an informed decision about how to proceed with your claim.

WHAT DOES A PERSONAL INJURY ATTORNEY DO?

You may be wondering what a personal injury attorney does, after the attorney is retained to represent the client in an accident. First, the attorney may assist you in getting your vehicle repaired in a timely fashion, since insurance companies may be difficult to deal with if your vehicle needs to be repaired quickly and properly. For most people, quick repairs are necessary to take the children to school and get to work. Your attorney could help you find a rental vehicle while your vehicle is being repaired, or help you recover "loss of use" funds to cover the monetary value for the number of days your vehicle is out of service (due to repairs). Some people are unaware that they can obtain this type of compensation.

Your attorney may also be able to help you recover your lost wages or a percentage of your lost wages if you are out of work due to your accident. In Florida, PIP will pay 60% of lost wages up to the PIP cap—other states may be different. An attorney can help you prioritize PIP benefits so that you receive the applicable and necessary benefits: lost wages, payment of medical bills (with a cap of $2,500 for non-emergency or $10,000 for an emergency medical condition), reimbursement for mileage, etc.

A personal injury attorney will research and notify you of special liens that may need to be paid from the proceeds of settlement, including these: Medicare, Medicaid, Workers' Compensation, health insurance, or medical payment insurance. An attorney can negotiate these liens to reduce the amount that must be paid from your settlement proceeds. Your attorney will make sure that those liens are not missed because, if you do not pay those liens from your settlement proceeds, the companies (and especially the government) will pursue you to collect the amounts due. You do not want to receive a letter a year or two after you have settled your claim, demanding money for payments made under Medicaid or Medicare.

Personal injury attorneys can also advise your spouse of his or her rights with regard to the accident, such as filing a "loss of consortium" claim to collect damages for your spouse. This would be due to the fact that the accident caused your spouse to take on a larger family workload because you were unable to perform tasks as you once did before the injury. Also, if the insurance company is not working to settle a claim within the policy limits, which would have been settled by a reasonable person, the attorney can file a civil remedy notice, or a "bad faith" claim. If an insurance company is found to be acting in "bad faith," then the insurance company could be found liable for damages in excess of the available insurance policy limits. For example, let's say that your uninsured/underinsured policy limits are $10,000, but your insurance company is not acting in good faith. If you prevail in the bad faith claim, you could potentially recover more than $10,000 by proving that the insurance company had the opportunity to resolve the case within the policy limits but failed to do so in a timely manner.

Another element of a personal injury attorney's job is to conduct a scene investigation. Either the attorney or someone on his behalf will go to the scene of the accident to take photographs and measurements because some things at an accident scene could have contributed to the accident, such as sight lines. There may be something that blocked your vision, such as hedges planted too closely to the corner, blocking the view of oncoming traffic. If an expert testifies that the county planted these hedges too close to the corner, or the hedges were in violation of a county code, then the county may have liability for the accident. That is why it is very important to view the accident scene to take note of the conditions, including blind spots, dips in the roadway, or other hazards. Pictures of the accident scene sometimes reveal that the accident occurred not because of the negligence of one of the drivers, but because of the intersection's layout.

Your personal injury attorney will also assist you with pre-suit tools used for information-gathering by insurance companies, called "examinations under oath" or "recorded statements." In Florida, your insurance company has the right to take a statement under oath or examination under oath. You will be placed under oath and asked questions by the attorney for the insurance company or an investigator for the insurance company. It could take under an hour or more than a day, depending on the case. Your personal injury attorney can prepare you for this by telling you the type of questions to expect and by discussing any issues that may come up during the examination. The attorney will attend the examination with you to make sure you are treated fairly and to object to any inappropriate or overly repeated questions designed to get you to say the answer that the questioner wants to hear.

Part of the job of a personal injury attorney is to gather and review medical records and PIP logs in order to prepare a formal demand letter to the insurance company. This demand sets forth your attorney's argument on your behalf with the goal being to obtain the maximum monetary compensation to which you are entitled based upon the facts of your case. The demand letter typically will not be sent until you have completed your medical treatment and are ready to work toward a resolution of your claim. If the insurance company and your attorney cannot agree on a settlement, then your attorney will file a lawsuit to bring your case before a judge or a jury.

One very important role of an attorney is to find insurance coverage that is available to you. After an accident, the police officer will issue a report listing the parties involved in the accident and the insurance company for each vehicle. However, if an individual does not have an insurance card at the time of the accident, the officer may omit the insurance company on the police report. Your attorney will investigate to determine if there is any potential insurance for the vehicle, even if the police report did not reflect a company name. This might be as simple as contacting the DMV or as complex as hiring an investigator to contact the person who caused the accident to obtain the relevant insurance information. There are multiple means and programs that can be used to obtain insurance information if you know where and how to look. Even if, after reading the police report, you think that there is no insurance to pay for your medical costs and pain and suffering, an attorney may be able to find insurance to cover your injuries and provide compensation for your losses.

Finally, attorneys offer legal advice and review all possible options so that you can make informed decisions about how to proceed with your claim. Advice can include whether or not a settlement seems fair, or if more money may be obtained for your claim. Obviously, there is no guarantee one way or another as to a jury's decision if the case goes to trial. However, an experienced attorney can tell you what this type of case usually obtains as an award, based on jury verdict reports and his own years of knowledge and experience.

THE INSURANCE COMPANY HAS NO INCENTIVE TO BE FAIR OR TO FULLY COMPENSATE YOU FOR YOUR LOSS

Having a personal injury attorney representing your interests from the beginning of the case benefits you because you are in an adversarial position with the insurance company. First and foremost, an insurance company is in business to make a profit, not to pay all of the presented claims in the full amount demanded by the injured party. The adjuster's job is to save money for the insurance company—his job may depend upon how much money he is able to save the company. An adjuster is typically judged by how much he pays on claims. If he pays out too much in claims, he may be facing a review by his supervisor. This automatically places the adjuster in an adversarial position with the injured party because the adjuster is looking out for his job rather than the best interests of the victim.

Adjusters use various tactics when dealing with an injured party. One approach is for the adjuster to act as if he is your best friend, building rapport to make you feel comfortable and secure. In conversation, he may say, "Hey, you don't need any attorney. We could just resolve this here and now, between you and me." He will then make you a settlement offer that is probably far below the actual worth of the claim. Keep in mind that the adversarial position between you and the insurance company means that they are never your friend. Their job is to preserve the assets of the insurance company by paying the least amount of money for each claim.

Another approach used by adjusters involves intimidation. In some situations, an insurance adjuster will accuse the injured victim of being at fault in the accident, when he knows that is not the case—or he accuses the victim of fraud. The adjuster may say, "Hey, this property damage doesn't match up; therefore, we don't think this accident truly occurred." Obviously, the adjuster is simply trying to save the insurance company money by scaring the victim into giving up the claim. The injured victim may begin to believe that pursuing a claim is not worth the trouble and aggravation, even though he knows that his injury was a result of the accident. He may feel too nervous or intimidated to pursue the claim. An attorney can hire an accident-reconstructionist to determine if the accident really did cause this damage. The accident-reconstructionist will use measurements of the skid marks, expert evaluations of the vehicles, and other evidence to determine that the accident did occur and that fraud did not.

Another tactic used by insurance adjusters is to rush the injured party to sign a full release before any medical tests are performed. This saves the insurance company money in medical bills and settles the claim before the injured person realizes the seriousness of the injury. For example, the adjuster may try to get a release before an MRI is performed. Without an MRI or other applicable diagnostic tests, you may not know the severity of your injury, such as a herniated disc, a torn rotator cuff, a fracture, etc. Adjusters will also push you to give a recorded statement right after the accident. However, in most states, the at-fault party's insurance company cannot compel the injured party to give a pre-suit statement, recorded or otherwise. Insurance adjusters will ask you to provide a statement by making it sound as if you are required to do so.

Unfortunately, once you have provided this statement, they will use it to lock you into your testimony. The main problem with giving a statement soon after an accident is you may not be fully concentrating on the questions and might give inaccurate testimony. Once it is memorialized on tape, you are stuck with it unless a plausible explanation is provided. Furthermore, you may not feel the pain from injuries immediately after the accident due to your state of shock, and may not for several days. However, if the adjuster asks you right after the accident and you answer, "No, I am not in any pain," the insurance company will use that against you later in your case. Most people wake up stiff and in pain a day or two after an accident.

Only when they go to their doctor do they realize that they have been seriously injured. In Florida, your own insurance company is entitled to take a statement from you, such as the examination under oath mentioned earlier. That is one of the tools used by insurance companies to evaluate a case or to try to make a case go away through intimidation. You are in an adversarial position with the insurance company and its representatives from the first moment after an accident occurs through to the end of your case.

NAVIGATING A PERSONAL INJURY CLAIM

When navigating a personal injury claim, there are many things that you must take into account. First, there are deadlines that must be met or your claim could be barred. Second, criteria must be met before you are entitled to benefits such as personal injury protection or insurance coverage for vehicle repairs. You really need an attorney to help you navigate those complexities. Some states, such as Florida, are "no fault" states. What that means for you is that if you are in an accident, your own personal injury protection (PIP) insurance will pay for your medical bills. They pay for the first 80% of the medical bills. If you have medical payment coverage, that will pay the remaining 20% of the bills. Many people who move to Florida from a state without this policy may wonder why their insurance company had to pay their medical bills when they were not at fault. One of the main reasons for enacting this policy is that the Florida legislature wanted an injured party to have the means to seek necessary medical treatment, regardless of whether or not they caused the accident. For example, an individual who causes an accident, unintentionally but through negligence, has the funds available to seek medical care even if they do not have health insurance. In states without PIP coverage, such as Georgia, an injured person must use other avenues to have his or her medical bills covered after an accident. That is another complexity of personal injury cases—finding a way to cover your medical bills, especially early on in the case.

In some instances, you might be injured in an automobile accident without owning a vehicle, and therefore have no automobile insurance coverage. There are ways that you may still be covered through PIP. If you live with a vehicle-owning relative at the time of the accident, you may qualify for personal injury protection under that vehicle's automobile insurance policy, even though the vehicle was not involved in the accident. If you live alone or you do not live with any relatives who own a vehicle, you still may be able to receive compensation for personal injury protection to help with your medical bills from the insurance policy covering the vehicle in which you were a passenger. Your attorney will help you determine if you qualify for personal injury protection and assist you with filing the claims.

When a pedestrian is injured or a bicyclist is hit by a vehicle, you would first seek PIP through your own automobile insurance, if available, and then look to a relative's policy. If neither applies, you may think that there are no other avenues to pursue. However, certain case law states that when a pedestrian or bicyclist is injured by a driver, the driver's insurance company may be responsible for the payment of medical bills up to the limit of his personal injury protection coverage. That is another reason to have the help of an experienced personal injury attorney, so you can navigate the complexities and previously unknown options of your case.

Also, if you are involved in an automobile accident with an uninsured or underinsured driver you may believe that there is no hope for recovery. However, an attorney can help you file a compensation claim for injuries under your own uninsured/underinsured motorist coverage. This coverage provides an umbrella for you if the other driver does not have insurance or adequate coverage. What happens if you get into an accident without having purchased uninsured motorist coverage because your insurance agent never discussed that option with you? Under Florida law, you must sign a form that is called "Uninsured Motorist Rejection Form" or "Selection Form" stating whether or not you chose to purchase uninsured motorist coverage. If you did not sign this form, your attorney can assist you by filing a claim against your insurance company, requiring it to provide coverage for failing to properly inform you of your rights, and for failing to have you sign the proper documents. Therefore, the insurance company could possibly be liable even though you never purchased the coverage.

Stolen vehicles are another complexity. For instance, if someone steals a vehicle and then causes a motor vehicle accident, most of the time the insurance company for that vehicle would not be required to pay damages because the person took the vehicle without permission. Most insurance policies have clauses requiring the driver of the vehicle to have received permission from the owner of the vehicle, be it actual or constructive consent, in order for that vehicle's insurance coverage to apply to an accident. For example, if the owner of the vehicle left the keys out in the open, and the owner had not stopped the driver on several previous occasions from taking the keys and the ve-hicle, implied consent could be argued. Therefore, the insurance company may be responsible for payments under the policy.

Regarding Workers' Compensation immunity, let us imagine that you are a delivery person working for a trucking company and get involved in a car accident. However, the accident is caused by another employee of your company. You may only have the right to file a Workers' Compensation claim. On the other hand, if you are working and involved in an accident caused by another driver unaffiliated with your company, you may be able to file both a Workers' Compensation claim and a personal injury claim. That person's personal injury claim typically would not be barred by Workers' Compensation immunity, and his insurance company could be required to provide compensation, if all the criteria are met for a bodily injury claim.

LANDMINES THAT CAN SINK YOUR CASE

When handling personal injury cases, attorneys often encounter landmines that could potentially be detrimental to the client's case, such as a statute of limitations. Essentially, you only have a certain period of time to bring your claim, or you are forever barred from bringing the claim. You never want to be barred from seeking compensation for your injuries, and it's important to consult with an attorney early on in the case regarding deadlines, which vary by state. In Florida, with few exceptions, the statute of limitations is four years for a negligence action such as an automobile accident. Other states may have shorter limitations, such as the two-year limit in California, though deadlines can change. A Floridian involved in an accident in California may believe that he has four years to bring a claim, but the California statute of limitations will apply since the accident occurred in California.

Another landmine may include certain criteria that must be met to receive your full PIP benefits. Florida recently passed legislation stating that, in order to receive the full $10,000 in PIP benefits, you must have what is called an "emergency medical condition." You must consult with a certain specialist, such as an M.D. or a D.O., and have them give an opinion as to whether you have suffered an emergency medical condition requiring treatment. Without an emergency medical condition, the insurance company could cap the PIP benefits at $2,500. Prior to the new legislation, you could seek medical treatment months after the accident and still receive PIP benefits. However, you must now seek medical treatment within 14 days of the accident or forfeit your PIP benefits.

There are also litigation deadlines. If you miss a deadline to answer interrogatories (written questions) or fail to appear at a deposition, the court could impose sanctions that would severely hurt your case. People who represent themselves in a pro se manner for an automobile accident run the risk of missing deadlines and having sanctions imposed, such as striking your claim or being ordered to pay attorneys' fees for the opposing party.

Deadlines even exist with your own insurance company. If you do not report the automobile accident to your insurance company within a reasonable period of time, your insurance company could potentially deny your claim. Most insurance companies have an "examination under oath" clause, and if you fail to appear, you could be deemed in violation of your insurance policy. Most insurance companies also have what is called a "cooperation clause" within their insurance contract, stating that you must cooperate with your insurance company's reasonable requests, such as the examination under oath. If you fail to appear for an examination under oath, the insurance company could void your insurance contract. Without a valid reason, this would be sustained even under a challenge in court.

In medical malpractice cases, landmines also exist with the statutes of limitations. In Florida, as in most other states, you have a shorter statute of limitations (two years in Florida) for medical malpractice cases than in regular negligence cases. Yet sometimes an attorney may be able to extend the medical malpractice statute of limitations to two years from when you knew or should have known of the malpractice, with a maximum of four years from the date of the malpractice.

Even if you are able to bring the medical malpractice claim, many requirements must be met in order for you to be successful. Some states require affidavits from experts in the same medical specialty before you can even file a lawsuit for medical malpractice. Many times, those affidavits are difficult to find. It is difficult to find a doctor who shares the same general location and medical specialty with the target doctor and is willing to put his name on an affidavit. Many are completely unwilling to get involved. In most cases, you must go out of the area or out of state to find an expert willing to review the file and provide an affidavit. Some states have what is called a "pre-suit screening period" for medical malpractice cases. This is a window of time in which the doctor and his insurance company can perform informal discovery, which could include requests for documents or interrogatory questions. You are required to submit to this informal discovery and are barred from filing a lawsuit until this window has passed and you have completed pre-suit mediation. If you are not experienced in medical malpractice cases, going forward with a lawsuit during this window could prevent you from taking your claim to court.

Another landmine opens up when a person makes a statement— of any type. Whatever you say can be used against you at a later date, even statements made at the scene of an accident. For example, it is human to apologize for an accident, even if you did not cause it. This could be brought up later in the case, when the insurance company wants to allege that you admitted fault. This commonly occurs in lane merger accidents, when no one is really sure who caused the accident, but one of the individuals may apologize out of politeness. The insurance company will use this apology as a way to prove that you thought you were at fault. This is an exception to the hearsay rule because you made the statement directly to the defendant.

TAKE ADVANTAGE OF YOUR FREE CONSULTATION

If you do decide to consult with an attorney, it's important to know that most consultations for personal injury cases are free. Bring all of your documents with you to the consultation: medical bills, the police report, insurance information, pictures of the accident scene, pictures of injuries, and other items related to the accident. The attorney will review the documentation to determine if you have a case and whether it is a case that you have a mutual interest in pursuing. I typically sit down with my potential client and review the information with him to advise him as to whether I believe he has a case or not, or whether more information needs to be gathered and reviewed prior to making a final decision. At this time, I invite the potential client to ask me questions. You should ask the attorney about his experience, his background, whether he handles only personal injury cases or other case types, and if he goes to trial or settles most cases. If he handles other types of cases in addition to personal injury, ask him what percentage of his cases are personal injury cases. With respect to my firm, I have been practicing law, concentrating in personal injury cases, since 1996. As a former insurance company attorney, I have represented many of the insurance companies in the past. I have worked with most of the large insurance companies and their adjusters, so I know what they typically look for when evaluating a personal injury claim.

Regarding automobile accident cases, I know the red flags that the insurance companies typically look for and how they will evaluate a case. I use that knowledge to assist my clients with the claims process, as we proceed to attain the best possible settlement. For example, in a significant accident case or with a questionable injury, the insurance company may hire a private investigator to obtain videotape evidence about your habits. I explain to my clients that if they are claiming to be unable to do something and are later found to be engaging in that activity, there is a good chance that they will be caught on tape. It is better to be honest and say that you can do something but with pain, rather than simply stating that you cannot do the task at all. For example, "I am still able to pick up groceries out of the trunk of my car but am now in pain when I do so," as opposed to saying "I can no longer lift groceries out of my trunk."

During a consultation, we will discuss your medical options and we will make sure that you are seeing the appropriate medical specialist for your type if injury. We have you provide us with the contact information and medical specialty for the doctor you are seeing so that we can contact that doctor to request your medical records and updates on your treatment and progress. We will discuss property damage options, vehicle repairs, which insurance company is responsible for the repair bills, and the quickest way to get the vehicle repaired. Sometimes this means going through the at-fault driver's insurance company rather than your own insurance company. If fault is an issue, the insurance company may want to investigate before agreeing to pay for the repairs. This could be a slow process, so you may be able to look to your own insurance policy if you have the correct coverage. You may be able to have your vehicle repaired more quickly through your own insurance policy, even if you have to pay your deductible. In that case, your insurance company will pursue the other insurance company to recover the cost of your deductible (which will be reimbursed to you) and the money your insurance company paid for repairs on your vehicle.

We will discuss all of your injuries during the consultation and we will take photographs of your visible injuries. In other words, if you were in a serious accident where the windshield shattered, causing cuts all over your body, there should be photographs usable for evidence. Lastly, all of the potential insurance coverage available to you will be explored so that we can determine which ones to pursue.

EXAMPLE OF WHAT A GOOD PERSONAL INJURY ATTORNEY CAN DO FOR YOU

While writing this chapter, the case of a young woman who was injured in a minor car accident comes to mind. We will call her Jane. Jane was in a motor vehicle accident with minimal property damage. This low-impact accident caused less than $500 in property damage to her vehicle—nothing much could be seen except for a broken license plate. However, Jane suffered a significant neck injury that required surgery. The surgery was performed by a very conservative surgeon with a reputation for only performing surgeries that were absolutely necessary. Jane had consulted with two other law firms prior to seeking our assistance. The case was nearing the statute of limitations, after which time she would be barred from making a claim. The second attorney declined the case, stating that the insurance company would not make an offer; it was felt that the injury was not caused by this low-impact accident because there was very little property damage. Jane was referred to our office by a family member previously represented by our firm whose case had good results. Jane was told during the initial consultation that it was going to be a difficult fight, which she knew after being rejected by two other law firms. We had to act quickly to file the lawsuit prior to the expiration of the statute of limitations.

We went through the typical depositions, and Jane was a very credible witness. She explained that she never had neck problems prior to the accident. After the accident, she began having neck problems, and an MRI revealed a herniated disc. She went to a conservative doctor because she was not trying to "build a case," she was just trying to get better. The doctor recommended surgery, and Jane followed his recommendation. Our argument was, "but for" this accident Jane's surgery would not have been necessary. The insurance company kept fighting, stating that the facts had not changed; no offers had been made with the previous two attorneys, and the insurance company would not make any offers now. We were able to have Jane see another medical expert who, after reviewing her records and performing an examination, came to the same conclusion as the conservative doctor: the surgery was a result of injuries sustained in the accident.

We retained a biomechanical engineer to review the evidence and facts of the case. This expert had impeccable credentials and had testified as a defense expert witness on behalf of insurance companies in the past. Said expert came to the conclusion that the subject injuries and subsequent surgery were caused by the accident in question.

We contacted the insurance company, explaining that we were prepared to call the biomechanical engineer as an expert witness at the trial to explain that the neck injury and surgery were caused by the accident in question. We further explained that we believed that the jury would side with us, given the expert's testimony. The insurance company agreed to resolve the issue without taking the case to court, and we were able to obtain a satisfactory settlement for our client.

Contacting an attorney right after an accident includes a great advantage: it does not cost you anything. Even if you do not want to pursue the case, talking with an attorney can reveal your legal rights and preserve the future option of pursuing a case. You should photograph everything and keep a diary to record your pain, comments made by other parties, things that you are unable to do because of your injury, memories about the accident scene, and other useful information relevant to your accident and injury. Memories fade, so having a diary is an excellent way to jog your memory at a later date, if the case moves toward a trial.

PURCHASE THE RIGHT INSURANCE COVERAGE

With respect to insurance coverage, carry as much automobile insurance as you can afford. State minimum requirements are just not enough. This does not necessarily mean purchasing a $1 million policy, but I would recommend having the largest amount of coverage that you can reasonably afford to protect yourself. You do not want someone coming after your personal assets because you did not have sufficient coverage to pay for their injuries and damages. Purchasing uninsured/underinsured motorist coverage (UM) is also a good idea because this protects you in the event that someone without sufficient insurance coverage or assets causes you a significant injury. You could be stuck with medical bills totaling six figures if the other party does not have insurance or assets and you did not purchase UM coverage.

Most importantly, do not sign anything with an insurance company before first having an attorney review the documents. Consult with an attorney so that you know what you are signing and your legal rights, even if you do not plan on pursuing a claim. Do not be afraid to talk to your attorney if you have questions during your case. Your attorney is there to help you navigate the claims process and protect your interests, so you can receive just compensation for your injuries.

(This content should be used for informational purposes only. It does not create an attorney-client relationship with any reader and should not be construed as legal advice. If you need legal advice, please contact an attorney in your community who can assess the specifics of your situation.)

10

WE MUST HOLD
COMPANIES AND
INDIVIDUALS
ACCOUNTABLE FOR
THEIR CONDUCT

by John M. O'Brien, Esq.

John M. O'Brien, Esq.
John M. O'Brien and Associates
Elk Grove, California

John M. O'Brien is a Sacramento-based personal injury attorney with over 24 years of legal experience and an AV peer review rating from Martindale-Hubbell, a distinction granted to only 5% of all lawyers. Mr. O'Brien is recognized throughout the California legal community for his zealous and effective representation of individuals who have been catastrophically injured. Since its inception in 1996, his firm, John M. O'Brien & Associates, P.C., has obtained numerous multi-million dollar jury verdicts and settlements in a wide variety of personal injury cases. Mr. O'Brien is a member of the American Board of Trial Advocates (ABOTA), American Association of Justice, Consumer Attorneys of California and Capitol City Trial Lawyers Association (CCTLA). In 2009, the CCTLA awarded him with the distinction and honor of being its Advocate of the Year and in 2014 Mr. O'Brien was recognized as a "Super Lawyer" by peers in Northern California.

WE MUST HOLD COMPANIES AND INDIVIDUALS ACCOUNTABLE FOR THEIR CONDUCT

It is an honor to accept the responsibility for representing people who have been injured or have suffered a tragic loss. Personal injury attorneys are indispensable—not only to their clients, but also to the public. Holding individuals and companies responsible for negligent conduct or damages caused by defective products not only provides monetary compensation for the injured person, but also sets important societal standards. Minimum safety standards are often set by juries deciding whether certain conduct should be acceptable. Without this accountability, a higher number of individuals would probably be injured or killed because of unsafe products on the market. The same holds true for keeping companies and individuals accountable for their conduct. If drivers did not suffer civil consequences for injuring others because of distracted driving, speeding, or drunk driving, there would be less social incentive to avoid injurious conduct. By holding companies and individuals accountable for negligence and careless or reckless acts, personal injury attorneys are performing a service that benefits everyone.

During my initial consultation with a prospective client, the first item on the agenda is to determine whether they even need a lawyer. Occasionally, I will advise some people to handle their own cases, especially minor automobile accidents involving a simple visit to the emergency room, or a few visits to a chiropractor. Such cases can be handled more efficiently in small claims court without an attorney. However, even a case in small claims court involving only minor injuries can be difficult for someone who is unfamiliar with the legal system. The claimant must still prove that the defendant was negligent or irresponsible in the operation of the vehicle. He must also provide evidence of medical expenses, lost wages, and proof of pain and suffering. All of this must be articulated to a judge. For some, these tasks may prove too daunting.

A personal injury attorney should always be retained for complex cases that involve serious injury or unclear liability on the part of the defendant. An experienced personal injury attorney will understand all aspects of the relevant law that applies to the case, including the rules of evidence, and will know how to prepare the case effectively for trial. Successful personal injury cases that are expertly prepared to go to trial most often result in the claimant receiving fair value for his injuries. An insurance company will not respect the claim, the claimant, or the claimant's attorney if it does not believe that the lawyer is ready, willing and able to go to trial. Being fully prepared to go to trial gives the insurance company more incentive to treat your client fairly.

YOU MUST PROVE YOUR CASE

Every aspect of preparing a case for trial is complicated, because you must be able to prove your case according to the rules of evidence and the pertinent law. Proving liability can be an extremely complicated undertaking. In a product liability case, for example, experts must be retained to examine every aspect of the product's design and manufacturing, to show why the product was defective, and to prove that the product did not perform as safely as an ordinary consumer would expect. In some instances, you may have to provide alternative designs that are safer than the defective product. Since most consumer products involve technical and complicated designs and manufacturing processes, you must have expert testimony to prove your case. In many automobile defect cases, the number of experts needed to figure out how or why a component malfunctioned in an accident can be daunting. For example, in a case where there was a defective airbag, understanding the airbag's design, the software that tells the airbag when to deploy, and all of the moving parts that must work for airbag deployment is a complex matter that requires investigation and expert testimony. This is just one element in a complex process of proving liability before holding a defendant accountable for an injury, which is why the assistance of an experienced personal injury attorney is so vital.

In addition to liability, you must also prove that the defendant's conduct or the defective product caused the injury to the claimant. Again, using the defective airbag case as an example, you must prove two things: that the airbag was defective, and that the person's injury was caused by that defect. Therefore, if you have someone who sustained a head injury or neck injury, you would need to hire a biomechanical engineer to testify why the injury would have been less serious or nonexistent had the airbag deployed correctly.

Even if it's proven that the defendant is liable for the client's injuries, you must then prove the extent of the injuries and their economic cost. This often involves a team of experts (including physicians, rehabilitation experts, and economists) that must evaluate and testify as to the damages sustained by the client. Physicians who treated the client before the lawsuit was filed must also be included with the experts who were hired specifically for the litigation. When you view a personal injury case from the perspective of preparing for trial, proving the existence of all of the elements necessary to win at trial, and understanding how all of those things must come together under the rules of evidence, you can see why a complex personal injury case is not something to navigate on your own.

As a personal injury attorney, I must evaluate each case to determine if it can be won—if liability can be clearly identified, or if I think a jury will agree that the defendant should be held liable. This involves investigation beyond the police report, on my part and by my investigators, including interviewing eyewitnesses to get a more accurate and detailed accounting of what they would say at trial. Since police reports can be inaccurate, I must know exactly what a witness will say at trial to decide if I can prevail on the liability issues in the case. In some cases, liability is presumed (i.e., rear-end auto accident cases). In other cases, liability must be proven (i.e., both drivers swear they had the green light). In cases where liability is not clear, eyewitness testimony becomes a crucial factor at trial; jurors might discount each driver's perspective and give more weight to an objective eyewitness's account of the accident.

Therefore, learning what each eyewitness will say on the stand is absolutely necessary when evaluating a personal injury case.

During my initial evaluation, I also review the person's damages when determining if I will accept a personal injury case. I listen to what the person is telling me about sustained injuries to determine credibility, or if there is any exaggeration. I need to be engaged and believe what I am being told before becoming anyone's advocate. I do not want to feel that I am being misled in any way, since a jury will probably sense the same thing during trial. I advise my clients to be completely honest and not to exaggerate or try to make their injuries seem worse than they are; that is the worst thing a client can do in terms of appearing credible in front of a jury.

The third thing to be reviewed is the person's pre-existing conditions. For example, when I am litigating a car accident case involving injuries to the neck or lower back, a person's pre-existing neck or back injury and their treatment becomes extremely important. Again, I emphasize to my clients that they must be honest and forthright about any pre-existing conditions, because any mischaracterization can impact the plaintiff's credibility; especially when she is discussing the injury's effect on her life. Testimony must be consistent about the conditions of her life prior to the injury, and what it's like after the injury. This testimony must also be consistent with information reported to physicians and other healthcare professionals over the years.

These are just some of the things a good personal injury attorney will review during the initial consultation and investigation. The reason an individual retains a personal injury attorney is to recover damages and find some type of justice.

When I accept a personal injury case, I want to be sure that I can prevail when providing this service for my clients.

PERSONAL STATEMENTS – A WAY FOR INSURANCE COMPANIES TO MINIMIZE THE VALUE OF YOUR CLAIM

Personal injury attorneys must deal with insurance companies on a daily basis. One of several possible problems involving insurance companies can be clients' statements given prior to hiring the attorney. Giving a statement is inevitable when an accident occurs. For example, in an automobile accident, you must give a statement to the police officer responding to the accident scene. In a slip and fall case, you will often give a statement to a store manager, insurance adjuster, or investtigator when they contact you to gather more information about what occurred. Everything that a person says to anybody related to the accident could potentially be brought up later in settlement negotiations or at trial, and there will be accountability for what was said at that time.

Due to the requirement to give statements to police officers or others, statements need to be as accurate as possible. People have a human tendency to downplay the pain that they are experiencing after an accident. In slip and fall cases, embarrassment often keeps people from being completely honest about their level of pain. They simply want to get out of the store as quickly as possible, and may not want to admit that they suffered a fractured wrist or a back injury. Also, the adrenaline caused by an auto accident often masks symptoms until the shock of the accident begins to wear off. Due to adrenaline, most people will not begin to feel the overall soreness and the pain from neck and back injuries until several hours after the accident or even the next day. Most immediate responses after the accident will be: "I am fine," or "I am not hurt," when they really are injured. Later, insurance companies and defense lawyers will use these statements against the plaintiff at trial. My advice to anyone is to be very careful when giving statements or making any comments about an accident. What you say can and will be used against you later. Be accurate and honest and consult a personal injury attorney as soon as possible after the accident.

These personal statements are the reason why insurance companies work quickly to obtain a recorded statement after an accident. That way, they can take advantage of any changes in your description of how the accident occurred, changes in how you describe your injuries, or other discrepancies in your statement. The insurance company will argue that you were not being truthful when you made the statement or when you made the changes. Inevitably, when a personal injury attorney is retained, the person must provide sworn testimony through a deposition. This could be up to a year or more after the accident occurred, so of course there are going to be some discrepancies in descriptions given months later. Again, the insurance company will try to exploit any differences in testimony as a way to prove the person is not credible. I counsel people not to give statements to insurance companies. The only reason for the insurance company to take a statement, is to use your words against you to try to minimize how much they have to pay at the end of the case. Minimizing claims is the sole goal of an adverse insurance company—it does not have your best interests in mind when contacting you. These companies are working for their insured customers, not for you.

DON'T DEPEND ON SOMEONE ELSE'S INSURANCE TO COVER YOUR CLAIM

The topic of insurance companies brings to mind something that I repeatedly handle: automobile accident insurance issues. In California, the statutory minimum for liability insurance is $15,000. If you are in an automobile accident caused by a driver holding only the state minimum coverage, you may be left with thousands of dollars in unrecoverable damages because the person at fault only had $15,000 in coverage. The first step is to make sure you understand your own insurance policy coverage and limits. Uninsured and under-insured motorist coverage is standard in every California policy, and is usually the same amount carried for your liability insurance. For this reason, I recommend that people carry the highest uninsured motorist limits they can afford. If you are involved in an automobile accident that is not your fault and the other driver has minimum policy limits, your underinsured coverage will cover what is lacking in the other driver's insurance.

For example, if you are injured in an accident and suffer a significant injury, such as a herniated disk in your neck that requires surgery, the minimum coverage of $15,000 carried by the defendant will be far below your actual treatment costs. Therefore, we would recover the $15,000 from the third party policy and then turn to your own insurance company to pay for the balance of your damages up to your policy limits. Having a high limit for uninsured and underinsured coverage is important; even with $100,000 of coverage, this will probably not be sufficient to cover damages associated with a herniated disc. Treatment and interference with the enjoyment of your life will probably exceed even your own insurance limits in such a case, but it is better to have at least some protection than to have nothing at all. I stress to all of my clients that they should discuss these coverages with their insurance company and increase limits whenever possible to avoid situations like these.

Another type of automobile coverage that's very helpful in personal injury cases is the Med-Pay or "medical payments provision" in some policies. With a Med-Pay provision, liability or fault-finding does not matter; your insurance company will reimburse you for out-of-pocket expenses related to the accident up to the amount of coverage, which is typically $5,000. This helps cover your health insurance deductible and co-pays when seeking treatment for your injuries. If you have no health insurance, having this safety net as part of your automobile insurance policy can help with getting necessary treatment after an automobile accident. Again, I counsel my clients to take advantage of this standard policy provision because it is often a very small addition to their overall premium.

People often wonder about why certain parties are named in a lawsuit when a personal injury case is filed. One common assumption is that if the insurance company does not settle out of court, that the insurance company will be sued. This is not the case—you must sue the driver of the vehicle that caused your injury. The insurance company is not named as a defendant in the lawsuit. If the case goes to trial, the jury is never told that the person does or does not have insurance. The insurance company will provide the driver with an attorney to defend the case, and the insurance company will pay the settlement (or judgment) up to the amount of the policy limit, if you win the case. This is also true with respect to a product liability case, or premises liability case. The actual defendant that caused the injury is sued, not the insurance company. Even though the insurance company may ultimately be liable to pay damages under its insurance contract with the defendant, it is still not named when filing a personal injury lawsuit.

CONTINGENT FEE AGREEMENTS MAKE THE SYSTEM ACCESSIBLE FOR EVERYONE

Most people also ask about the attorney's payment for services. In most cases, a personal injury attorney takes cases based on a contingency fee. That means that the attorney will not charge for any of his time or for costs advanced in the case until the case is resolved. Along with the client, the attorney is taking the risk of winning the case by advancing costs associated with preparing the case for trial, and performing casework without being paid. The attorney is not paid until he wins the case or obtains an agreeable settlement for the client.

Contingency fees are fairly standard in personal injury cases. Most attorneys will charge a one-third contingency fee if the case is settled prior to trial. If the case goes to trial, the fee will rise to 40% to cover the additional costs and time associated with taking a case to trial. Personal injury is one of the few types of law for which attorneys consistently charge fees based on a contingency arrangement. This is a benefit for clients, because most people suffering from a catastrophic injury are also suffering from the devastating financial effects associated with the accident and injury. They are not able to pay an attorney a retainer fee to be billed at an hourly rate, or to advance all of the costs involved with a case. Contingency fees give equal court access to people from all socio-economic classes, not just those who have the means to pay an attorney's retainer fee for work performed on an hourly basis.

Boating Accidents

Automobile accidents are not the only type of personal injury cases handled in my practice—I also work with cases involving injuries sustained while boating. Boating is a recreational activity that is fraught with many unknown and unanticipated risks and dangers, and many different scenarios have resulted in minor to serious personal injuries. Some common types of boating accidents can involve a driver who is not paying attention, or is not experienced in handling a boat under certain conditions. I have handled cases where the driver was traveling too fast for the area, hit a submerged object, and caused injury to everyone on board. Several boating accident cases involve defects in component parts of the boat; such as when an outboard motor's steering mechanism failed at a high rate of speed, causing a violent 90-degree turn that ejected everyone from the boat. I have also seen cases where the accident was caused by a commonly used boating product such as a towable tube or wakeboard.

After accepting a boating accident case, I know that the case will likely require a number of experts in a variety of different fields. For example, in the case involving the steering mechanism on the outboard motor, I retained a marine engineer to inspect the failed motor component, as well as an expert in boating safety operations who investigated other potential causes for the violent 90-degree turn. With both of these experts working on the case, the most likely causes of the serious and catastrophic injuries suffered by my client were narrowed to the failure of the steering mechanism. While expensive and complex, this process was shown to be completely worthwhile after we were able to prove that the steering mechanism was at fault and caused the injuries to my client.

Boating accident cases often reveal careless or reckless behavior (because people forget that boats can be dangerous), as well as impairment by alcohol or drugs. In California, there has been a vigorous campaign to educate the public that operating a boat while intoxicated is just as serious as driving a car under the influence. Personally, I have seen a decrease in the number of alcohol-related personal injury cases, but it is still one of the major factors in many boating accidents. People are getting the message that alcohol and boating do not mix. However, there are still those who will overindulge and cause an accident, especially because boating is a highly recreational activity.

GETTING TO KNOW THE VICTIM

One of the biggest challenges faced by a personal injury attorney is the representation of an individual (or the family of an individual) who has sustained life-changing injuries or has been killed as the result of an accident. The attorney has a solemn duty to see that the defendant is held accountable for his actions and to achieve some measure of justice for this person or family. Some jurors have expressed doubt that a monetary reward will somehow repair the damage when the injuries sustained are irreversible, or the person was killed. However, the process of going through the trial and holding the reckless or careless party responsible is cathartic for the injured person or the family of a deceased victim.

Often I will spend as much time as I can with the victim or his family, usually at their home, learning about their lives before and after the accident. We collect everything we can, from awards and scrapbooks to pictures and videos, which reveal the life led by the person before the accident. I will also spend time with the friends of a victim to learn everything about that person's life, because a jury needs to hear these details to be able to evaluate the impact of the injury on a person's life. It is up to the attorney to convey the story of the event and the level of catastrophe to the victim, through his family, friends, and co-workers. As an attorney learns more about the victim's life before the accident, it becomes personal to him and he can relate that to the jury. Even if the case does not go before a jury, an attorney must still convey this information to an insurance adjuster, either in settlement negotiations or in a mediation setting, to resolve the case. The attorney must convince this person, who probably handles hundreds or thousands of cases each year, why this case is special, and why a jury is likely to find this person's plight particularly moving. This often means that the attorney must find ways other than simply relating the facts to demonstrate the impact of the injury on the victim.

I have used day-in-the-life videos as a way to demonstrate a person's damages. For example, a person who has suffered a catastrophic injury who is now a quadriplegic cannot even feed himself. I must relate how having a life care plan is necessary to ensure there is enough money to take care of the basic needs of this person for the remainder of his life. He will probably never do anything as he did before, and a minimum life care plan is the only way to give that person some quality of life. This also helps answer the questions that jurors may have about why it helps to award money in these cases, even though it cannot "undo" the accident or the injury; money will give that person some semblance of a normal life in terms of caregivers or environment modification. In many cases, only a jury verdict awarding damages for the injury will make this possible. Representing someone who has suffered a devastating, life-altering injury is one of the most important aspects of what I do as a personal injury attorney.

PRODUCT LIABILITY CASES

Out of all the personal injury cases handled by my firm, I find product liability cases to be the most fascinating, probably because of my undergraduate studies in economics and the fact that strict liability is imposed for a defective product in California. By strict liability, I mean that a victim is not required to prove that the defendant manufacturer did anything wrong, that its actions were negligent, or that the manufacturer fell below the standard of care required during manufacturing. A manufacturer is strictly liable for any defective product that it produces and markets which causes injury to a person. Strict liability requires only that we prove that the product was defective and that the defect caused harm to a person.

The consumer expectation test is one way to prove that a product was defective. This test simply requires a finding that the product did not perform as safely as an ordinary consumer would expect. With strict liability, there's no need to prove that the manufacturer was negligent or that its conduct was reckless or careless. It's only necessary to prove that the company manufactured the product, sold that product, and that someone was harmed due to a defect in the product. The company is then strictly liable for the damages caused by the product.

Strict liability is not absolute liability. We still have to prove that a defect in the product caused harm, but we are not required to prove that the manufacturer should have conducted more research or taken other steps that would have prevented the injury. It is sufficient to prove that the product's defectiveness caused injury to a person and did not perform as safely as an ordinary consumer would expect. From a societal perspective, an injured person should not bear the burden of an injury or loss when a manufacturer of the product that caused the injury is making a profit from distributing and selling the product to consumers. The company is in a better position to bear the burden of loss than the innocent consumer who simply purchased the product, expecting that it would perform in a safe manner. This is why strict liability is used in a product liability case instead of a negligent or fault-based liability standard. The manufacturer is reaping the benefits from the sale of its product and should accept the consequences when that product injures someone.

Another aspect of product liability cases deals with the concept of "failure to warn." A product may not have a defect in its design or in its manufacturing process but still be considered defective because the company failed to warn consumers or give proper instruction as to the product's use. This aspect of product liability is unique in personal injury litigation, in that it provides another way to hold manufacturers responsible for injuries sustained from the use of their products, when adequate instructions for the product's use were not provided. In a product liability case, the manufacturer is not the only entity that can be held accountable. Every person or company in the stream of commerce from wholesalers to retailers of the product can be held accountable for damages.

One complication in some product liability cases is due to the fact that so many products are being manufactured outside of the United States. Holding foreign companies accountable can be a difficult undertaking for a personal injury attorney. For example, obtaining jurisdiction over a Chinese company that may have used below-standard materials in its product is very difficult. Fortunately, in many cases, it's possible to hold accountable a domestic company used somewhere in the product's distribution or manufacturing process. This is an example of why our product liability laws are like a "net" over the entire manufacturing and distribution process. In our example of the product produced in China, there is probably an American company that is used to distribute the product to consumers in the United States. Hopefully, this American company is adequately capitalized or has adequate insurance against the type of loss that can be caused by a defective product. An attorney will look for an American distributor or other local connection when searching for parties to hold accountable for a product that was manufactured by a foreign company.

A PRODUCT LIABILITY CASE YOU WILL NEVER FORGET

One of the most interesting product liability cases I have handled occurred a few years ago. It dealt with a product that was designed to help patients experiencing swelling after an injury. This cryotherapy unit was designed much like an Igloo ice chest with a tube attached to it. The tube was attached to a rubber bladder that was placed around the injured body part. The patient filled the chest with ice and water. When the unit was turned on, the ice water was pumped through the tube to the bladder placed around the injured body part providing a circulating ice pack to treat the injury.

My client had routine surgery to repair a torn ligament in his ankle, and his surgeon recommended that he use the cryotherapy unit to reduce pain and swelling after surgery. The surgeon relied on the company salesman to explain to the patient how to use the unit. Unfortunately, the salesman was rather young and new to the company. He advised my client to use the product 24/7 until he returned for his first post-op visit four days later. My client and his wife listened to these instructions and followed them to the point of setting alarms so they could replace the ice and water every eight hours around the clock. My client had near-freezing water circulating around his foot and ankle for four days. Upon meeting with my clients for the initial consultation, I expressed my disbelief that the salesman instructed them to use the machine non-stop for four days. They then told me they were also given written instructions, and produced a bullet-point instruction sheet that actually advised them to use this device "24/7" for four days until returning for the post-op visit!

Of course, when you have near-freezing water circulating around your foot and ankle for four days you are likely to develop a cold injury. By the time he returned to his physician, my client had one of the worst cases of frostbite imaginable. He had to endure numerous medical procedures to remove the blackened sections of his foot that were killed by the frostbite, followed by amputations performed on two toes and a section of his heel. He also developed a Methicillin-resistant Staphylococcus Aureus infection (an antibiotic-resistant infection present in many hospitals known more commonly as MRSA) that almost took his life. My client missed the birth of his daughter and the first six months of her life because of this infection. More surgery followed as the surgeons tried to save the foot with skin grafts from his stomach and thigh, but he eventually had a below-the-knee amputation. There were two more amputations because of problems with the residual stump. Each time, my client had to endure the painful process of getting used to a prosthetic attachment, since scar tissue and a callus must develop in order to use the prosthetic.

Unfortunately, that was not the end of my client's injuries. He endured several treatments for the MRSA infection, including chemotherapy, which destroyed his immune system causing him to contract the H1N1 virus. Again, my client was near death several times as he was treated for MRSA and H1N1. This was the most unbelievable odyssey of pain and suffering I have ever witnessed—all caused by what seemed to be an innocuous product that was meant to help this 28-year-old man after a simple surgery. His life was changed forever due to the careless instructions given by a 22-year-old recent college graduate, improperly instructing my client on the use of the cryotherapy unit. This is an example of a product that was not defective in its design—the product did exactly what it was designed to do—but it caused injury because of a failure to warn or give proper instructions for use.

ONE CARELESS DECISION – KILLS TWO

Another personal injury case concerned a young man who was traveling with two of his friends on their way to Monterey. As they drove down highway 156, unbeknownst to them, a truck driver ahead of them had experienced a flat tire on his trailer. After contacting his employer, the truck driver decided that it would be far more convenient to deal with the flat tire by returning to the previous exit with a rest area and restaurant, rather than waiting on the side of the road for assistance.

To return to the previous exit, the truck driver decided to execute an illegal U-turn across a two-lane highway, and then cross the dirt median to enter oncoming traffic in the fast lane going in the other direction. He did this from the shoulder of the highway with less than 600 feet of sight distance between the truck and approaching traffic. Believing that everything was clear, the driver began to pull an 18-wheel truck and rig out onto the highway to perform the illegal U-turn. My client and his two teenage friends were making their way around the curve to encounter what seemed like a truck just normally pulling out from the shoulder into the slow lane of traffic. They continued to approach the truck at normal freeway speed.

Instead of simply merging into the slow lane, the truck continued across into the fast lane leaving my client's vehicle without any room to maneuver. Evidence showed that the driver of my client's car hit his brakes and tried to veer to the left, but that put the car directly into the area where the truck was performing the U-turn. The car submarined under the side of the trailer, shearing off the car's roof and killing the driver and my client, the front seat passenger. The rear seat passenger suffered a catastrophic brain injury. This was a tragic case caused by a horribly negligent and careless truck driver. Fortunately, we were able to hold the truck driver and his employer responsible for all the suffering they caused that day. This one careless decision cost two lives and forever changed the life of the third person. Holding companies and persons accountable who cause tragedies like this one and the one I described before make me proud to be a personal injury attorney.

(This content should be used for informational purposes only. It does not create an attorney-client relationship with any reader and should not be construed as legal advice. If you need legal advice, please contact an attorney in your community who can assess the specifics of your situation.)

www.ingramcontent.com/pod-product-compliance
Lightning Source LLC
Chambersburg PA
CBHW070306200326
41518CB00010B/1917